To Paul,
Happy holidays!

THE NUTCRACKER *Sweet*

Also by Linda Hymes:

The Dancing Gourmet: Recipes to Keep You on Your Toes!

The Dancing Gourmet presents

THE NUTCRACKER *Sweet*

SHOW-STOPPING DESSERTS INSPIRED
BY THE WORLD'S FAVORITE BALLET

Linda Hymes

with photography by Derek Gaffney

Lindergaff Books
San Francisco

Published by Lindergaff Books, LLC.
698 DeHaro St. Unit A
San Francisco, CA 94107
(415) 285-2912
www.dancinggourmet.com

Cover photo: Chocolate Mousse King Cake photo: ©2004 by Derek Gaffney.
Backdrop photo : ©2003 Stephan Laurent, courtesy of Ballet Russes Scenery Collection of Butler University, Indianapolis, Indiana of backdrop from the ballet *The Magic Swan*, designed by Eugene B. Dunkel. Premiere in New York, on October 13, 1941, by the Ballet Russe de Monte Carlo.
The Magic Swan was a one-act ballet choreographed by Alexandra Fedorova, reconstructed from divertissements in the third act of Petipa's *Swan Lake*.
Our sincere thanks to Stephan Laurent and Butler University for permission to reprint photo from their Ballet Russes Scenery Collection.

Cover design, art direction, layout and food styling: Linda Hymes
Copy editor: Rebecca Pepper

All photography ©2004 Derek Gaffney except cover photo of backdrop:
© 2003 Stephan Laurent

Special thanks to Jean Weaver, Marianna Gebara and the Board of Directors of Nutcracker of Middle Georgia, Inc. All performance photos ©2003 Derek Gaffney of Nutcracker of Middle Georgia, Grand Opera House, Macon, Georgia (pp. 2,10-11, 16-17, 26-27, 29, 36-37, 52-53, 78, 106-107, 131).
Sets designed by Bobby Berg.

Thanks also to Bruce Stievel of Nevada Ballet Theatre for permission to photograph. All performance photos ©2003 Derek Gaffney of Nevada Ballet Theatre, Las Vegas, Nevada (pp. 40-41, 54-55, 74-75, 98, 120-121).

Character illustrations on pp. 12, 19, 49, 58, 65, 69, 76, 93, 96, 105, 114, and 128 by Noah D. Gelber.
For further information about Noah or to contact him via email, please visit his website at http://www.noahtheartist.de/

Library of Congress Cataloging in Publication Data
Hymes, Linda
      The Nutcracker Sweet : Show-Stopping Desserts Inspired by the World's Favorite Ballet / Linda Hymes: photographs by Derek Gaffney and others; photo styling by Linda Hymes.
         p.   cm.
      Includes Index.
      ISBN 0-9719782-1-2
      1. Baking 2. Cookery 3. Ballet 4. Chocolate 5. Performing Arts. I. Title.
      2004093537

PRINTED IN HONG KONG

First Edition
10 9 8 7 6 5 4 3 2 1

SAN: 255-0709

Contents

$\mathcal{P}$reface

$\mathcal{T}$he Nutcracker is the most well known of all classical ballets and probably the most popular holiday performance throughout the world. When I was a dancer, it was always my most anticipated annual treat—with the elaborate costumes and that magical, timeless music, the season wasn't complete without it. From the first rehearsal to the last performance, being in the Nutcracker let me revel in the two things I was most passionate about: dance and desserts.

I have always loved to dance this ballet, yet it wasn't until I turned back to the original story as a chef that I discovered E. T. A. Hoffmann had quite a sweet tooth as well—in fact, his original story, *The Nutcracker and the King of Mice*, is all about desserts! Through the fanciful imagination of a young heroine named Marie and a fabulous cast of confectionary characters, he celebrates the most coveted desserts of the 19th century, many of which don't always appear in the ballet. In Hoffmann's tale, we are introduced to gingerbread men and a marzipan castle, shortbreads and macaroons, sugared fruits and Krakatuk nuts, and a town called Bonbonville. There is a king of chocolate, a prince of Almonds and beautiful swans floating on lemonade, and in the populous city of Sweetmeatburg, there stands a lofty cake covered with sugar where it is the pastry cook (not the Sugarplum Fairy) who reigns supreme. Thanks to his story, the ballet has left visions of sugarplums dancing in our heads for almost two hundred years. I think Hoffmann would be pleasantly surprised to find that his confectionary fantasy is celebrated in over 500 Nutcrackers performed in the United States each year. It is to him and to all those who bring this great ballet to life that I dedicate these recipes. Enjoy, and please support the arts.

The Ballet (in a nutshell)

On the stroke of midnight in the town of Nuremberg, we are ushered into the magical world of Marie Stahlbaum's fantasies, where good battles evil and true love conquers all. Our young heroine, Marie, steals downstairs before going to bed to fetch the new Nutcracker doll her godfather, Herr Drosselmeyer, has given her at the family's annual Christmas party. Exhausted from the excitement of the evening, she falls asleep under the sparkling lights of the tree. All is quiet, then out of the cracks scurry scores of menacing battle mice. Marie wakes in horror as their leader appears, a giant seven-headed Mouse King who has come to slay her beloved Nutcracker. In defiance, she throws her slipper at him, allowing the Nutcracker to cast a fatal blow. He then changes into a handsome prince and off they go through the snow to paradise–the Land of Sweets.

Attention to Detail

(a note on the recipes)

When the young Russian choreographer George Balanchine was asked in 1934 to head what would later become the New York City Ballet, his response was "Yes, but first a school." Proper technique is the fountain from which creative juices flow, whether referring to Balanchine's desire to sculpt dancers for his company or the more immediate subject we are discussing here: choreographing the final course to a meal. Keep in mind a few basic culinary principles and you can master a multitude of sweet treats that will leave visions of sugarplums dancing in your head. This being said, a measure of artistic license is allowed–feel free to vary or make substitutions to these recipes. For example, the Champagne Poached Pears will be just as delicious if made with summer-fresh, firm peaches or nectarines. If it is the middle of winter and blood oranges are available, let them adorn your panna cotta instead of ordinary navels.

If you don't fancy citrus fruit, nestle your pudding in a puddle of blackberry coulis or shower it with some sliced strawberries. Instead of Sugarplum Sauce, the Vanilla Soufflé can be served with a sauce made of a purée of berries, soft, ripe mango or persimmon. Follow the tips below to ensure that you end up with the creation you envisioned.

1. Read through the recipe completely before you begin, so you have a good idea of the steps involved and the time required for preparation.

2. Be sure to have all the ingredients measured out and the tools needed handy before you begin the recipe. *Mise en place* is the culinary term for proper preparation and is as important in baking as it is in cooking. Laying out your prepared ingredients before you begin putting them together helps you keep from forgetting important steps like adding the baking powder to the flour or mixing in the cream of tartar while whipping the egg whites. Mise en place also helps save energy because your oven won't sit waiting while you go rummaging for your baking pans, and your caramel sauce won't burn while you look for the cream.

3. Don't be put off by what looks like fancy dessert footwork: the more elaborate recipes in this book only look difficult to make. A show-stopping finale can often be reduced to an easily manageable project if you treat the recipe as a compound arrangement of fairly simple components, many of which can be done in advance. I find entertaining much less stressful when I know the dessert course is done and dusted before dinner has even

begun. The benefit of most cakes is that they require no last-minute fiddling–just slice and serve. Cake layers can be made in advance and frozen, and icings and fillings can often be made days in advance and then returned to spreading consistency shortly before assembling the final cake. The Grand Finales chapter includes many such impressive do-ahead extravaganzas: both the cake layers and the buttercreams in the Chocolate Symphony and the Prince of Almonds Torte can be made and frozen for up to several weeks as long as they are tightly wrapped. Just thaw to room temperature before assembling. Buttercreams may need to be briefly rewhipped until smooth and spreadable before using.

No-bake choices for elegant endings can also make entertaining easier. For the Champagne Poached Pears, both the ice cream and the chocolate sauce can be made ahead, and store-bought ice cream can always be substituted for homemade.

If Swan Lake will make the perfect ending to your gala evening, prepare the choux pastry ahead of time and store the baked pieces in a tightly sealed container. You can whip the cream at the last minute and assemble the swans quickly with the aid of a pastry bag.

If the only exercise you want at dessert time is slicing and serving, bake up the Raspberry Linzertorte or the Dark Chocolate Pearly Tart early in the day. The Pear and Hazelnut Marzipan Tart tastes even better the day after it is made. And if any baking at all is more effort than you can muster, make a simple panna cotta. Both the espresso and classic versions stand elegantly on their own, served in a beautiful glass with a shaving of chocolate or inverted onto a plate and topped with fresh fruit. Remember that a successful dessert isn't about slaving away to master the perfect balance of butter and sugar, just as every ballet doesn't have to close with a virtuosic show of thirty-two fouettés. Often, in baking as in dance, less is more–sometimes the simplest effort turns out to be the most beautiful.

4. Be aware that oven temperatures can vary dramatically from the number set on the dial. If your oven has not been calibrated (even if it is brand new), you might want to buy a small oven thermometer and leave it on the rack, out of the way of your baking pans. Baking times are meant to be guides and are therefore not absolute, so it is a good idea to always test for doneness with a toothpick prior to the baking time specified in a recipe rather than assuming that your oven will take exactly the amount of time specified.

The temperature of your oven can also vary from front to back and side to side. If you notice that one side of your tray of cookies is browning more quickly than the other, switch the tray around halfway through the baking time.

5. Unless otherwise specified, all eggs are large, sugar is regular granulated, and butter is always unsalted.

Act I begins in the home of Dr. Stahlbaum, where the family's annual holiday party is just beginning. A great tree stands majestically in the center, with candles hanging from its branches and shiny boxes wrapped with ribbons surrounding the base. The house fills with guests, and they drink and dance and eat wonderful confections like light as air Blackberry Dewdrop Charlotte and celestial Lemon Meringue Angel Roulade filled with tart lemon curd. The maids pass the sweets on silver trays, carrying tiny porcelain cups filled with raspberry-studded chocolate pudding and rich crème brûlées covered with sparkling sugar crusts. Light and airy Vanilla Soufflé with Sugarplum Sauce satisfies Mrs. Stahlbaum, and the Marzipan Castle Pudding crowns the evening, served with a traditional white hard sauce.

Light as Air Entrechats
and Pudding Variations

Vanilla Soufflé with Sugarplum Sauce 18

Espresso Panna Cotta 21

Panna Cotta with Orange 22

Toasted Coconut Crème Brûlée with Irish Cream 24

Pumpkin Crème Brûlée Tarts 30

Spanish Hot Chocolate 31

Chocolate Raspberry Tea Cups 32

Chocolate Fondue 34

Panettone Pudding 38

Cranberry Apricot Cobbler
with Oatmeal Nut Streusel 39

Marzipan Castle Pudding 42

Tiramisu 45

Lemon Meringue Angel Roulade 46

Blackberry Dewdrop Charlotte 49

Vanilla Soufflé with Sugarplum Sauce

People often get stage fright when it comes to serving soufflés, but the only tricky part is timing. You can make this recipe in stages, preparing the pastry cream base and Sugarplum Sauce a day in advance, then whipping up the egg whites while your guests are finishing off the wine. Everyone will be ready for dessert just as the soufflé comes out of the oven.

SUGARPLUM SAUCE

4 cups diced, pitted ripe plums

¼ cup sugar, or to taste

2-inch strip lemon zest

¼ teaspoon black peppercorns, tied in a small piece of cheesecloth

½ cup water

SOUFFLÉ

2 tablespoons sugar

1 tablespoon cornstarch

2 tablespoons flour

6 large eggs, separated

6 tablespoons superfine sugar

1⅓ cups milk

1 vanilla bean, split lengthwise

¼ cup heavy cream

powdered sugar, for dusting

1. MAKE THE SUGARPLUM SAUCE: Combine the plums, sugar (the amount of sugar you use really depends on the sweetness of the plums, so adjust the sugar to taste), lemon zest, and pouch of peppercorns in a medium pot. Cover wit the water and bring to a boil. Lower the heat and cook gently for about 10 minutes, stirring occasionally, until the fruit is soft. Remove the strip of lemon and the peppercorns, then pour the fruit into a blender. Blend until smooth. Let cool. Serve warm or at room temperature.
Makes about 2 cups.

2. MAKE THE SOUFFLÉ: Heavily butter a straight-sided 1-quart soufflé dish. Toss in 2 tablespoons sugar and shake to coat the inside of the dish.

3. Cut a sheet of parchment paper large enough to wrap around the rim of the dish and high enough to extend 3 inches above the rim. Fold the sheet in half to make it more sturdy, then butter and sugar one side. Wrap around the outside lip of the soufflé dish with the sugared side on the inside, and tape or tie it so it stays secure. Set aside.

4. Preheat the oven to 350°F.

5. Sift together the cornstarch and flour. Beat the egg yolks with 4 tablespoons of the superfine sugar (reserving 2 tablespoons to beat into the egg whites) until thick and light, then whisk in the cornstarch mixture.

6. In a medium pot, bring the milk to a simmer. Scrape the seeds from the vanilla bean into the milk, then toss in the whole bean. Turn the heat to the barest bubble and let the vanilla infuse for 10 minutes. Remove the vanilla bean and discard (or pat it dry and stick it in your sugar bowl), then stir in the heavy cream. Let cool.

7. Whisk the infused milk into the beaten egg yolks, then pour the mixture back into the pot. Cook over medium heat, stirring constantly, until thickened like pudding. Transfer to a bowl and press some plastic over the surface. Set aside for at least 15 minutes.

8. When the custard has cooled to room temperature, whip the egg whites to soft, loose peaks. Sprinkle in the remaining 2 tablespoons of superfine sugar and keep beating until stiff. Gently fold in the custard, then transfer to the prepared soufflé dish.

9. Place the dish on a baking tray so it will be easier to remove from the oven, then bake for 20 to 30 minutes, until puffed and golden brown. Dust with powdered sugar and serve immediately, accompanied by the sugarplum sauce.

Italian panna cotta, or "cooked cream", is the current dessert cart darling in restaurants, but it is so easy to prepare that it is also a perfect dessert to make at home. Suitable for any season, it is little more than sweetened cream set with gelatin. The result is a mousselike texture that is lighter and more refreshing than a flan or crème caramel. In this recipe, espresso enhances the light creamy flavor, like a latte pudding. You can serve it turned out of ramekins onto dessert plates or in decorative stemmed glasses. Be sure to measure the ingredients exactly, though—panna cotta should quiver gently when nudged with your finger.

1 cup cold whole milk

2¾ teaspoons unflavored gelatin

⅓ cup plus 2 tablespoons espresso or very strong coffee

½ cup sugar

pinch of salt

3¼ cups heavy cream

vegetable oil spray

Chocolate sauce, such as Thinner Chocolate Ganache (page 142), for serving (optional)

1. Pour the milk into a medium pot. Sprinkle the gelatin over the surface and let it sit for 5 minutes, until the gelatin softens.

2. Add the espresso, sugar, and salt and place the pot over medium-low heat. Stir gently until both the sugar and gelatin have dissolved. Remove from the heat and stir in the heavy cream.

3. Divide the mixture among six 6-ounce ramekins that you have first sprayed lightly with vegetable oil spray. Cover with plastic wrap and chill for at least 4 hours or overnight, until set. (Alternatively, pouring the mixture into decorative dessert glasses will save the step of turning the panne cotte out onto plates, since they can go directly from the refrigerator to the table.)

4. To unmold the ramekins, slip a thin knife along the edge of each panna cotta to loosen it, then unmold them onto dessert plates. If you like, garnish with a swirl of chocolate sauce.

Panna Cotta with Orange

PANNA COTTA

½ cup low fat (2%) milk

2½ teaspoons unflavored gelatin

½ cup sugar

2½ cups heavy cream

1 teaspoon vanilla extract

ORANGE SAUCE

2 tablespoons sugar

2 cups fresh orange juice

3 seedless oranges

1. MAKE THE PANNA COTTA: Prepare six 4-ounce ramekins by spraying with vegetable oil cooking spray. Set aside.
Pour the milk into a medium pot and sprinkle the gelatin over the surface. Let stand for about 5 minutes, until the gelatin softens, then stir in the sugar. Place over medium heat and stir until the sugar and gelatin have completely dissolved. Remove from the heat. Add the heavy cream and vanilla extract and mix well. Divide the mixture among the oiled ramekins and cover with plastic wrap. Chill until set, at least 4 hours or overnight.

2. MAKE THE ORANGE SAUCE: Combine the sugar and orange juice in a small pot. Bring to a boil. Stir until the sugar has dissolved, then continue to cook until reduced by half. Let cool.

3. PREPARE THE ORANGE SEGMENTS: Trim the tops and bottoms from the oranges and cut in downward motions along the peel on all sides, so the pith and rind are removed. Cut in between the membranes with a sharp knife to remove the segments. (The culinary term for this technique is to "supreme.") Set aside.

4. TO SERVE: Unmold the panne cotte by dipping the base of each ramekin in hot water for a few seconds. Run a knife in a smooth, continuous motion around the edge of each ramekin and invert onto dessert plates. Arrange the orange segments around each panna cotta and serve with the sauce spooned over them.

There are as many variations of panna cotta as there are of the Dance of the Sugarplum Fairy, but this is one of my favorites—simple and elegant, with the citrusy freshness of ripe oranges combined with the smooth creaminess of the custard. They are like an elegant twist on an old-fashioned creamsicle. For a stunning contrast in color, replace the navels with blood oranges.

Toasted Coconut Crème Brûlée with Irish Cream

⅓ cup unsweetened flaked coconut

2 cups plus 2 tablespoons heavy cream

1 teaspoon vanilla extract

5 egg yolks

⅓ cup granulated sugar

2 tablespoons Irish cream liqueur

4 teaspoons granulated sugar (or demerera sugar),

4 sprigs mint, for garnish (optional)

1. TOAST THE COCONUT: Preheat the oven to 400°F. Spread the coconut out on a baking tray and place in the oven until lightly toasted. Watch closely—coconut burns very quickly! It will take only a minute or two to crisp to a golden brown. Remove from the oven and let cool.

2. PREPARE THE CUSTARD: Reduce the oven temperature to 300°. Place the cream in a medium saucepan and bring just to a simmer, then remove from the heat and stir in the vanilla.

3. Set another bowl containing the egg yolks and sugar over a pot of simmering water and whisk until thick and lightened. (Or use a hand-held mixer to beat the mixture over the simmering water.)
Pour a little of the cream through a fine-mesh sieve into the egg mixture and stir well. Gradually add the remaining cream, pouring through the sieve, and whisk until fully incorporated. Stir in the coconut and Irish Cream liqueur and set aside.

4. Place four 6-ounce ramekins in a casserole dish large enough to hold them snugly, then divide the custard among them. Slide the pan onto the center rack of the oven. Fill the casserole with hot water halfway up the sides of the ramekins, taking care not to spill water into the custards.

5. Cover the pan loosely with foil and bake for about 40 minutes, or just until the edges are set and the center wiggles tremulously.
Turn off the oven and leave the custards in the oven for 20 minutes more with the door ajar. Transfer the ramekins to a wire rack to cool completely. When they have cooled to room temperature, cover with plastic wrap and refrigerate for at least 4 hours or overnight.

6. MAKE THE CARAMEL CRUST: Just before serving, sprinkle 1 teaspoon of granulated or demerera sugar over the surface of each custard. Use a kitchen torch or the broiler to caramelize the top until it is crusty and golden brown. If you like, tuck a little sprig of mint in the edge of each ramekin before serving.

This recipe is inspired by a luscious crème brûlée served at the Oriental Club in London, where I worked while attending Le Cordon Bleu. It contains a hint of Irish Cream liqueur and lightly toasted coconut and is luxuriously exotic. Since the custards can be prepared in advance, they are well suited for holiday parties; just torch the sugar crust onto the tops right before serving. To prevent the surfaces from cracking, turn the oven off after baking and open the door. Let the custards cool slowly on the racks to room temperature before removing them from the oven.

The Grandfather Dance is just beginning, and it is time to put on my eyelashes. My makeup routine is as well-timed as a Swiss watch, only instead of the usual tick-tock, it is tuned to the tempo of Tchaikovsky's march. As with many baking techniques, the key to dancing well comes down to repetition, and putting on makeup is no different. "Mise en place" may be the culinary term for properly preparing ingredients before cooking, but it is also the recipe for a successful performance. I lay out my ingredients on my dressing table as methodically as though I was measuring butter, sugar, flour, and eggs, so they can be applied in their proper order, starting with cream and gradually adding color, then garnishing with a few strategically placed sparkles. The stage lighting and costumes are always the same, so without cosmetic improvisation, I can go from bareface to painted pearly in under fifteen minutes. A brisk Grandfather Dance means the conductor wants to move the show along quickly—

if tomorrow is Monday, he might be anxious for his day off. If I detect a barely discernible lilt in the timing, I must expect to balance notes and draw out the phrasing of the music to compensate for the relaxed conducting, which can be a by-product of a well-fed stomach. My toe taps to the music, gauging the speed, while I spread out multicolored tubs and tubes onto the dressing table.

In ballet companies, dancers always do their own hair and makeup. You may get the occasional wig in a gig with an opera company, but at the ballet there is rarely enough funding for such luxuries, so dancers are responsible for everything except fitting their costumes—this is the domain of the costume mistresses. These women are the faithful, the unseen and unheard martyrs of the ballet, underpaid seamstresses who pin, sew, and resew every costume in the show, from party dresses to angels' wings, to the rhinestone-studded tutu the Sugarplum Fairy must be hand-stitched into and snipped out of each and every performance to make sure the Cavalier's fingers don't get caught in the hooks during Grand Pas. A production of The Nutcracker often enlists an army of workers behind the scenes larger than the cast itself, doing the million and one tasks needed to make the show come together night after night. While parent volunteers police bon bons and toy soldiers, the older dancers are left to their own devices in separate dressing rooms far away from the children, where one can never rely on five-minute calls, and hair is put up and makeup is applied in ritualistic fashion, all the while breaking in new shoes, warming up cold calves, and sipping hot chocolate.

First comes the hair. If it's clean, this is a frizzy affair, requiring a generous handful of gel and some aggressive brushing to keep the wisps back. If not, a sleek slick-back is much easier: dirty hair for a ballerina means greater manageability. A rhinestone headpiece requires heavy-duty hairpins so it doesn't wobble or, worse, fly off during pirouettes. I remember one near miss that resulted from an inadvertent swipe by my partner's wrist. Despite being fortified with brand new Goody's, my tiara managed to become unhinged and I had to dance a good part of Snow Pas with one edge dangling like a pendulum back and forth across my forehead!

Now onto the face: both the size of the theatre and how much sleep you have had the night before will dictate how heavy-handed you are with the makeup sponge. If the stage is not equipped with a wide orchestra pit to separate you from the first row, then your average evening look with lashes will do. Matte foundation, but not a mask, blushing cheeks that don't look overly sanguine. Lips are colored to complement the costume and the role: lighter pinks for Snow Queen, rich and vibrant ruby red for Sugarplum, deep burgundy plum for Spanish and Marzipan. By mid-season, a new shade of lipstick can often be just the inspiration one needs!

Then come the eyes, which require strategically penciled black lines, as close to the lash line as possible, please. Now, this is harder than it looks, and if you have ever loitered around the stage door after a student recital, you will know what I mean. The lines must extend beyond the corner of the lashes so as to make the eyes appear bigger, yet not so far as to resemble the exaggerated stripes of a Kabuki actor.

Finally, the lashes. A good pair of falsies can last many seasons, glued on and pulled off over and over again, until they can comfortably be stuck on in seconds with a dot of transparent glue. A final smudge of iridescent vanilla shadow on the browbone, a spritz of perfume to mask the faint odor of a very expensive but rarely washed tutu, and it is time to warm up again before my entrance.

Nutcracker brings the art of pre-performance prep down to a science, a world where millions of props and performers must operate like a well-trained legion, standing in exactly the right place at the right time, both on stage and behind the curtain. Yet no matter how many performances one has under one's dance belt, there is always a special magic to dancing during the holidays, where everything in the world stops just for an instant as the first note of the overture is played. It is the magic of the Nutcracker, and is reflected in the eyes of the audience each time the curtain rises, making them hush and watch with wonder. For those of us onstage, what a rare and wonderful privilege it is to make that happen.

Pumpkin Crème Brûlée Tarts

TART SHELLS

2 cups all-purpose flour

1 tablespoon sugar

pinch of salt

¾ cup (1½ sticks) chilled unsalted butter, cut into tablespoon-sized pieces

1 egg, beaten

1½ tablespoons heavy cream

PUMPKIN CRÈME BRÛLÉE

1 can (15 ounces) pumpkin purée

¾ cup sugar

3 eggs

1½ cups heavy cream

¼ cup whole milk

1 teaspoon ground cinnamon

½ teaspoon ground ginger

¼ teaspoon ground nutmeg

pinch of ground cloves

¼ teaspoon salt

CARAMEL CRUST

about 3 tablespoons light brown sugar

1. MAKE THE TART SHELLS: Combine the flour, sugar, and salt in the bowl of a food processor. Add the butter in pieces and pulse until the mixture forms coarse crumbs. Mix the egg and cream and add to the mixture, pulsing only until the dough just holds together. Do not overwork or the dough will become tough. Gather the dough into a flat disk and pop it in the fridge for 1 hour.

2. When the dough is thoroughly chilled, cut it into 2 pieces and return one half to the refrigerator while you work with the other half. Roll the dough out on a lightly floured surface to a thickness of ¼ inch. Lay a 4-inch tart tin upside down over one edge of the dough and cut out a circle 1 inch larger in diameter than the tin. Press the circle of dough into the tin, using an extra scrap to push the edges into the corners so your fingernails don't tear the dough. Trim the edges by rolling the pin across the rim of the tin. Repeat with the remaining tart tins and dough—you should have enough for 10 tarts.

3. Place the tins on a baking sheet and line each shell with a small piece of parchment paper. Fill with beans or pastry weights. Chill for 30 minutes.

4. PREBAKE THE TART SHELLS: Preheat the oven to 375°F. Bake the tart shells for 8 minutes, then remove weights and parchment and bake 5 minutes more. Place on racks to cool. Reduce the oven temperature to 325°.

5. PREPARE THE PUMPKIN CRÈME BRÛLÉE FILLING: In a medium bowl, whisk together the pumpkin, sugar, and eggs until smooth, then add the cream, milk, spices, and salt and mix well. Pour ½ cup of the mixture into each tart shell.
Bake for 30 to 35 minutes, until the edges are set and the center barely jiggles. Let the tarts cool completely, then refrigerate for several hours or overnight.

6. MAKE THE CARAMEL CRUST: Just before serving, sift 2 teaspoons light brown sugar over each tart. Place under a preheated broiler (or use a small kitchen torch), and heat until the sugar sizzles to a rich brown. Let stand until the caramel hardens, about 1 minute, before serving.

Spanish Hot Chocolate

Nothing warms me up quite like hot chocolate when I'm backstage in a drafty theater. This recipe is quick and easy, travels well in a thermos, and works with any kind of chocolate. For an extra kick, add a splash of Frangelico liqueur in place of the cinnamon.

6 ounces best-quality dark or bittersweet chocolate, broken into small pieces
4 cups milk
pinch of ground cinnamon

1. Slowly heat the chocolate and milk together over low heat until the chocolate is melted and velvety smooth. Divide among 4 cups and sprinkle with cinnamon. Serve hot.

Make these little pumpkin crèmes brûlées to finish off a formal autumn dinner or when you want to jazz up the dessert course at Thanksgiving. The sugar crust adds crunch and sparkle. Keep the tarts chilled until you are ready to caramelize the sugar topping so the heat doesn't melt the custard underneath.

Chocolate Raspberry Tea Cups

Serves 6

Rich and sinful, these little cups are pure chocolate bliss. They are similar to the little French baked puddings called pots de crème, but are cooked on the stove rather than in the oven, so you are not limited to ovenproof ramekins for serving. Though preparing them this way calls for a bit more attention, requiring a slow, steady stir for a good 10 minutes, they can be made up to two days in advance.

1½ cups heavy cream

½ cup low-fat milk (2%)

1 vanilla bean, split lengthwise

3 extra-large egg yolks

½ cup sugar

5 ounces bittersweet chocolate, chopped

1½ teaspoons black raspberry or Chambord liqueur

6 ounces fresh raspberries

1. INFUSE THE CREAM AND MILK: In a medium pot, heat the cream and milk to a low simmer. Scrape the pulp and seeds from the split vanilla bean into the mixture. Give it a whisk, then turn the flame very low, just so the cream and milk barely bubble, and cook for another 5 minutes. Remove from the heat.

2. Place a large bowl that fits tightly over the pot of cream and milk and whisk the egg yolks and sugar until thick and pillowy.
Pour a little of the vanilla-scented milky cream (about ¼ cup) into the whipped yolks and whisk well, then gradually beat in the rest of the cream. Pour this mixture back into the pot and cook for another 10 minutes over very low heat, stirring continuously (this is important so you don't end up with a bowl of scrambled eggs), until the mixture thickens to a loose pudding consistency.

3. Remove from the heat and add the chocolate and raspberry liqueur. Stir until velvety smooth. Divide among 6 serving cups and let cool to room temperature. Poke 2 or 3 raspberries into the center of each cup, then chill in the refrigerator until set, at least 4 hours or overnight. Let stand at room temperature for 10 minutes before serving.

Chocolate Fondue

How appropriate that a simple bending of the knees is called by the same name as one of the most seductive of chocolate preparations! A softly melting bend of the knees, a fondue is a requisite barre exercise that, when correctly executed, shows two legs flexing and straightening at the same time, with one leg extended into the air. Relatively easy to do, you might think, yet like a simple demi plié, to master it can take an entire career. How well a dancer's fondues appear to melt largely contributes to resilient landings from jumps, supple and noiseless pointe work, and overall quality of movement.

It goes without saying that the chocolate you choose for a dessert fondue will repay you greatly if it is also of very good quality. For the best texture, flavor, and meltability, be sure to use a high-quality brand that you wouldn't hesitate to eat plain. Try domestic brand Scharffen Berger or imported Valrhona–both make deliciously fruity bittersweets, and Valrhona's white chocolate has a luxuriously buttery flavor without the pastiness that often occurs when melting inexpensive white chocolates.

Your basic fondue mixture is a snap to make, just chocolate and cream warmed together until velvety. Beyond that you have full artistic license; while I wouldn't go so far as to melt down a box of cordials, a deep, rich bittersweet chocolate combined with a fine-quality fruity liqueur makes a wonderful dipping sauce for pound cake and fresh strawberries, or, for a more elaborate dessert spread, provide a sampler of dipping choices: a selection of sauces, sliced bananas, oranges, and pineapple, graham crackers, macaroons, and buttery cakes cut into bite-sized cubes–pretty much anything that goes with chocolate will make your fondue proud.

FONDUE SAUCE

6 ounces dark, bittersweet, milk, or white chocolate

¼ cup heavy cream

1 tablespoon kirsch, amaretto, Frangelico, orange liqueur, or the liqueur of your choice (optional)

DIPPING CHOICES: ANY OF THE FOLLOWING

white chocolate macaroons (page 87)

8 ounces graham crackers, broken into squares

8 ounces marshmallows

pound cake or gingerbread, cut into cubes

maraschino cherries

fresh fruit: sliced bananas, strawberries, cherries, pineapple, clementines or oranges, pears, raspberries, grapes, etc.

1. MAKE THE SAUCE: Chop the chocolate roughly into little chunks. Place in a small pot with the heavy cream. Place over low heat and cook, stirring slowly but continuously, until melted and smooth.

2. Remove from the heat and stir in the liqueur if you are using it, then transfer to a heatproof bowl and set over a rack propped over a tealight flame (or use a fondue set).

3. TO SERVE: Spear the cookies, graham crackers, marshmallows, and/or fruit with fondue sticks or dessert forks and dip into the chocolate sauce. Eat quickly before they drip.

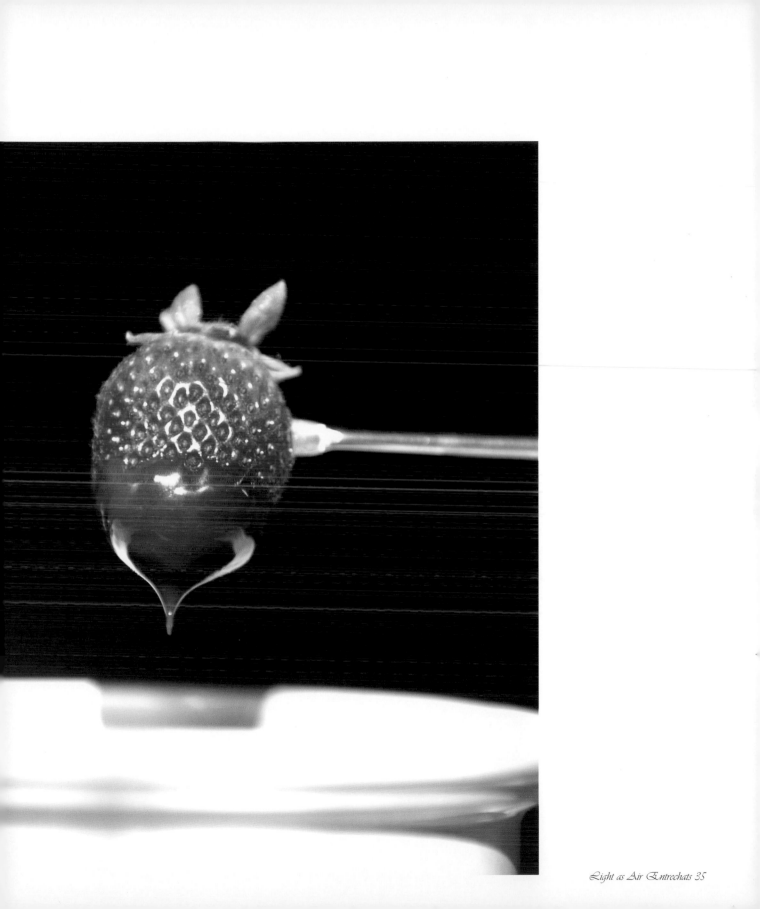

$\mathcal{M}$arie awakens to find her brother Fritz's hussars have come to life to help the Nutcracker battle the Mouse King's army.

Pannettone Pudding

1½ pounds stale pannettone, cut into cubes

2 cups whole milk

1½ cups heavy cream

4 eggs

¾ cup sugar

1 teaspoon almond extract

1 tablespoon butter, cut into small pieces

powdered sugar, for dusting

1. Preheat the oven to 325°F.

2. Tuck your hand into a small plastic bag and use it as a mitt to generously slather butter all over the bottom and sides of a 1½-quart oven-safe baking dish.

3. In a medium bowl, whisk the milk, cream, eggs, sugar, and almond extract together. Pile the cubes of pannettone into the buttered baking dish and pour the cream mixture over them.
Let sit for 5 minutes so the cake can soak up the liquid, then place the dish in a casserole filled with water. Dot with the butter.

4. Bake for 60 to 70 minutes, until the liquid is set and the top is golden and crisp. Let rest for 10 minutes before serving dusted with powdered sugar.

Italian pannettone reminds me of a cross between French brioche, English hot cross buns, and a refined fruitcake. It is rich and eggy and makes a great base for bread pudding.

Cranberry Apricot Cobbler with Oatmeal Nut Streusel

New York Times food writer Molly O'Neill once wrote that soup gives the body a sense of safety and satisfaction, but for me the best source of comfort after a long day can be found only in making something sweet. Baking without careful measurements or special ingredients is often the best way to relax and refuel, and for those times nothing fits the bill better than something slow-baking and unfussy, like a fruit casserole topped with sweet crumbs. Cobblers are great because they rely on ingredients like the slightly overripe fruit you usually have lying around the kitchen anyway, but the best thing about them is that they take so little effort in proportion to the pleasure they confer. Bright ruby cranberries and apricots are used here, but you can substitute any pie-friendly seasonal fruit you like, such as apples, plums, pears, or blackberries.

TOPPING

1 cup light brown sugar

1 cup old-fashioned rolled oats (not instant)

½ cup chopped toasted hazelnuts

¾ cup all-purpose flour

¼ teaspoon salt

½ cup (1 stick) chilled unsalted butter, cut into small pieces

FILLING

2 cans (15 ounces each) apricot halves in light syrup, with syrup reserved from one of the cans

1 package (12 ounces) fresh cranberries

2 medium Granny Smith or Pink Lady apples, peeled, cored, and cut into cubes

1 cup dried apricots, slivered

1 cup sugar

1. Preheat the oven to 375°F.

2. Make the topping first so it can chill in the refrigerator while you are preparing the filling: In a medium bowl, combine the brown sugar, oats, hazelnuts, flour, and salt and mix well. Cut in the butter with 2 knives or a pastry cutter until you have a coarse, pebbly mixture that clumps when you squeeze it together. Keep in the refrigerator while you make the filling.

3. MAKE THE FILLING: Cut the canned apricots into large chunks, then combine with the cranberries, apples, dried apricots, sugar, and reserved apricot syrup in a medium pot. Bring to a boil. Reduce the heat to medium and cook, stirring often, until the cranberries have popped and the apples have softened slightly, about 5 minutes.

4. Spoon the cranberry filling into a 13 by 9 by 2-inch baking dish. Sprinkle the streusel topping over the top.
Bake until the cranberry filling is bubbling through the crust, 25 to 30 minutes. Let cool for 5 minutes before serving with cream, whipped, or drizzled straight from the carton.

$\mathcal{T}$he original story of *The Nutcracker and the Mouse King* , written by E. T. A. Hoffmann in 1816, is far from the lighthearted production presented by most ballet companies today. In fact, the tale wasn't considered for a ballet until Ivan A. Vsevolozhsky, director of the Russian Imperial Ballet, read a revised version of the original story by the celebrated French author Alexandre Dumas père. With Dumas' sugar-coated interpretation, he saw the potential for a ballet and, along with Marius Petipa, his chief choreographer, commissioned the famous composer Peter Ilyich Tchaikovsky to write the music. When it premiered in 1892, the reviews were mixed: while the music was a big hit, the reaction to the ballet was less enthusiastic, but it continued to be performed in numerous restagings, eventually becoming what is today one of the world's most popular holiday traditions.

The first full-length performance of The Nutcracker in the United States was presented by the San Francisco Ballet in 1944, and it continued to gain popularity when George Balanchine created his production for the New York City Ballet in 1954. Having performed many of the roles himself as a child in Russia, Balanchine also based his ballet on the Dumas version, preferring a story line that showcased dancing rather than drama. Since its American debut, there has been a wide variety of new interpretations, both choreographically and musically, from Duke Ellington's pure jazz *Harlem Nutcracker*, composed in the 1940s,

to Mark Morris's *The Hard Nut,* set in the 1960s. The Nutcracker as a ballet came full circle in 2001, when the Kirov (formerly the Russian Imperial Ballet) presented an entirely reworked staging based on the original Hoffmann story. Designed by the Russian artist Mikhail Chemiakin, this most recent Nutcracker took a less fanciful and more psychological approach to the ballet, delivering a work of more substantive dramatic content than many previous productions. Currently more than 500 companies in America alone produce an annual Nutcracker, however, most present a happier and more family-oriented version. To keep attracting audiences, they continually add new flavor by presenting new costumes and characters or substituting alternate forms of expression for the classic ballet choreography, including skating snowflakes, choral singers, Roller-bladers, puppets, jugglers and cross-dressers.

A History of Nuts

Marzipan Castle Pudding

Almost every book on holiday baking in my mother's decades-old collection seems to include the requisite Christmas fruitcake. And appropriately so: it was the one gift you could count on during the holidays that would last all year, maintaining its lacquered-fresh look and taste no matter how long it was parked on the counter. In reality, it was an unappetizing, alcoholic slab of sticky, dark brown crumbs held together by equally stale-looking candied cherries, readily dismissed by friends and family alike.

I was first attracted to this very different cake primarily because it happens to be delicious. The name Marzipan Castle, though fitting for a recipe in this book (and the name of the ultimate destination of Marie and her Nutcracker Prince in Hoffmann's tale), actually refers to a traditional English cake known as castle pudding that is steamed in a large ornate mold. This version is the closest I come to making Christmas pudding because, like the anti-fruitcake contingency in Manitou Springs, Colorado, who have made an annual event of hurling their unwanted cakes into oblivion, I'm really not fond of most I've tried. Unlike all those artificially colored, shiny plastic-wrapped types, this version has neither candied fruit nor an infinite shelf life, and will not make a good doorstop. It is, rather, a very earthy steamed pudding, getting its sweetness from plump dried fruit and an appropriately Christmasy secret ingredient: nuggets of soft marzipan. I've replaced the usual brandy or rum with amaretto, a nutty and fragrant liqueur that echoes the flavor of the almond paste. Of course, if you miss the boozy taste, this cake is lovely accompanied by a good sherry or Cognac.

CASTLE PUDDING

3 tablespoons amaretto liqueur

¾ cup water

½ cup dried apricots, slivered

½ cup dried peaches or pears, coarsely chopped

¼ cup dried Mission figs, diced

1 cup chopped pitted prunes, diced

¼ cup black raisins

¼ cup golden raisins

½ cup (1 stick) unsalted butter, at room temperature

1 cup dark brown sugar

2 eggs

1 teaspoon grated orange zest

1 teaspoon grated lemon zest

2½ cups all-purpose flour

1 tablespoon baking powder

2 teaspoons ground cinnamon

1 teaspoon ground nutmeg

¼ teaspoon ground cloves

pinch of salt

1 cup milk

½ cup breadcrumbs

4 ounces marzipan, cut into small cubes

PUDDING SAUCE

¾ cup sugar

1½ tablespoons cornstarch

1 cup whole milk

¼ cup (½ stick) unsalted butter, cut into 4 pieces

1 teaspoon vanilla extract

On the way to the Marzipan Castle, the Nutcracker escorts Marie through magical pastures decorated with gold and silver fruit trees, flowers, and confections of all kinds. They enter through the Almond and Raisin Gate into Candy Mead, an enchanted meadow glistening with lights.

At the end of a mosaic path of colored candies, they come to Christmas Wood, where they pause to watch a ballet performed by sugar puppet shepherds and shepherdesses from the Wire Ballet Troupe, then continue on past the fragrant Orange Brook and River Lemonade, from which emanates the most delectable citrus perfume.

1. MAKE THE CAKE: In a medium saucepan, combine the amaretto, water, and dried fruit. Bring to a boil, then cover pan. Turn heat down to low and cook gently for 10 minutes. Drain off the liquid and set the fruit aside.

2. In a large bowl, cream the butter and dark brown sugar until light. Beat in the eggs, one at a time, then beat in the orange and lemon zests.

3. In a medium bowl, stir together the flour, baking powder, cinnamon, nutmeg, cloves, salt and breadcrumbs. Gradually beat into the creamed butter alternately with the milk. Stir in the cubes of marzipan and the cooked fruit.

4. Liberally butter an 8-inch decorative Bundt pan, and pour in the batter. Cover tightly with aluminum foil. Wrap with another layer of foil that is large enough to enclose the entire cake pan, and crimp the edges to form an airtight package. The cake will be steaming inside of a large Dutch oven, so make sure you have a pot large enough to fit the pan.

5. Place a rack, small can, or metal cup in the center of the base of the Dutch oven, then balance the cake on top. Fill with enough water to go halfway up the sides of the cake pan. Cover with a tight-fitting lid.

6. Bring the water to a boil, then lower the heat so the water boils gently and continuously, steaming the cake for 1½ hours. Replenish the water as necessary to keep the depth of water at a 2 inch level).

7. Remove the cake from the pot and gently unwrap the foil. Insert a knife into the densest part of the cake and test for doneness. Cool completely before serving.

8. MAKE THE PUDDING SAUCE: Place the sugar and cornstarch in a small pot. Stir in the milk and bring to a boil over medium heat. Keep stirring until thickened, 2 to 3 minutes.
Remove from the heat and whisk in the butter and vanilla. Let cool. Serve warm or at room temperature, spooning it over the pudding.

Most recipes for Italian tiramisu require that you refrigerate the layered dessert for several hours before serving, but I always find it makes the ladyfingers too soggy. Whipping the mascarpone and whipped cream together at the last minute gives it a fresher taste and, served in individual glasses, it is an elegant dessert for any post-performance party.

1 teaspoon instant coffee granules

8 ounces mascarpone cheese, at room temperature

2 egg yolks

1¼ cups powdered sugar

1 cup heavy cream

½ teaspoon vanilla extract

1 cup cold brewed coffee

¼ cup Kahlúa liqueur

7-ounce package lady fingers

3-ounce bar bittersweet chocolate

1. Place the coffee granules in a small plastic bag and crush to a powder with a rolling pin.

2. In a medium bowl, beat the mascarpone cheese with an electric mixer until light, about 10 minutes. Add the egg yolks and powdered sugar and continue beating for 2 to 3 minutes more, until light and fluffy.

3. In a separate bowl, beat the whipping cream and vanilla extract until stiff. Fold into the mascarpone mixture.

4. Combine the cold brewed coffee and the Kahlúa liqueur in a shallow dish. Cut the ladyfingers in half lengthwise and dip into the the coffee one to two seconds on each side, just until they absorb the liquid but not so long that they get soggy and fall apart. Place 2 ladyfinger halves in the base of a 6 ounce dessert glass, or you can use a 1 quart ceramic dish—just line up the soaked ladyfingers in a single layer. Top with the mascarpone mixture, spreading gently, then top with another layer of ladyfingers and mascarpone. Serve immediately or refrigerate for up to 3 hours.

5. To make the chocolate garnish, drag a vegetable peeler along the edge of the bar of chocolate and sprinkle the shavings over the top of the tiramisu. If the chocolate has been refrigerated, let it sit at room temperature for 10 minutes first so the shavings won't be too brittle and fall apart.

Lemon Meringue Angel Roulade

Act II opens in the Land of the Sweets, where angels carrying candles glide across the stage to light the way for the entrance of the Sugarplum Fairy. This snowy white angel cake is swirled with tart lemon curd filling and covered with snowdrifts of pillowy meringue.

ANGEL CAKE

⅔ cup cake flour

1 teaspoon baking powder

¼ teaspoon salt

9 egg whites, at room temperature

1 cup superfine sugar

1 teaspoon cream of tartar

1 teaspoon vanilla extract

LEMON CURD

2 eggs

4 egg yolks

½ cup plus 1 tablespoon sugar

½ cup freshly squeezed lemon juice

¼ cup (½ stick) unsalted butter, cut into small chunks

grated zest of 2 lemons

SWISS MERINGUE

3 egg whites, at room temperature

⅓ cup sugar

¼ teaspoon vanilla extract

1. MAKE THE ANGEL CAKE: Preheat the oven to 350°F. Line a 12 by 17 by 1-inch baking pan with a sheet of parchment paper.

2. Sift the flour, baking powder, and salt together. Set aside. In a large, spotlessly clean mixing bowl, beat the egg whites until they turn frothy and opaque. Add a few spoonfuls of the sugar and the cream of tartar, then keep beating at high speed until you've added the rest of the sugar and the egg whites are thick and lustrous. Sift the flour again over the egg whites and gently fold into the batter to incorporate. Spread the batter over the parchment-lined baking sheet and transfer to the oven.

3. Bake for 12 to 15 minutes, until the edges begin to turn golden and the center springs back lightly when pressed with your finger. Invert the cake onto a rack and gently peel off the paper while still warm. Let cool while you make the curd.

4. MAKE THE LEMON CURD: Combine the eggs, egg yolks, sugar, and lemon juice in a saucepan set over low heat. Cook, whisking constantly, for 6 to 8 minutes, until thickened to a pudding consistency. Remove from the heat and let cool slightly before whisking in the butter and lemon zest. Cool completely, then spread over the cake. Roll the cake gently into a cylinder.

5. PREPARE THE SWISS MERINGUE: Just before serving, whip the egg whites until you have soft peaks, then gradually add the sugar, beating until very stiff and glossy. Mix in the vanilla extract. Spread the meringue evenly over the rolled cake like a blanket of snow, then lightly burnish with a torch or place in a preheated 400° oven just until the meringue begins to brown. Serve promptly.

Blackberry Dewdrop Charlotte

The Dewdrop leads the corps in the Waltz of the Flowers, darting on and off the stage with lightning fast leaps and turns. In this vibrant finale, delicate ladyfinger cookies surround a tower of rich blackberry mousse like the petals of a flower.

The best thing about this cake is that it is deceptively simple to make. You'll need a 9-inch springform pan and for the whipped cream a pastry bag fitted with a star tip. A single-layer sponge cake bakes in the time it takes to prepare the blackberry mousse filling. The ladyfingers you can buy ready-made, so they need only to be trimmed and tucked in along the edge of the baked sponge. After several hours of chilling, just top the center with some downy dollops of freshly whipped cream and await the applause.

SPONGE CAKE

2 eggs, at room temperature

1 tablespoon plus ¼ cup sugar

½ teaspoon vanilla extract

¼ cup sifted cake flour

BLACKBERRY SYRUP

2 tablespoons water

3 tablespoons sugar

1 teaspoon blackberry liqueur or Chambord

BLACKBERRY MOUSSE

½ cup ice water

2 envelopes (4 teaspoons) unflavored gelatin

1 package (16 ounces) frozen blackberries, thawed

¾ cup sugar

2 cups heavy cream, chilled

TOPPING

1¼ cups heavy cream

2 teaspoons blackberry or raspberry liqueur

2 tablespoons powdered sugar, sifted

1 package (7 ounces) ladyfingers

1. MAKE THE SPONGE CAKE: Preheat the oven to 350°F. Butter a round of parchment paper and fit it into an 8-inch spring-form pan that has also been lightly buttered. Sprinkle in a spoonful of flour and shake the pan around to coat the bottom and sides evenly.

2. Separate one of the eggs, place the white in a medium bowl and beat until foamy. Add 1 tablespoon sugar and continue beating until stiff and glossy. Set aside.

3. In another bowl, beat the yolk and remaining whole egg with ¼ cup sugar until thick and lightened. Add the vanilla. Gently fold in the whipped egg white alternately with the cake flour. Spread into the prepared pan.

4. Bake for 10 to 12 minutes, or until golden and a toothpick inserted into the center comes out clean. If any batter sticks to the toothpick, pop the pan back in the oven for another minute or two, but watch closely because this cake cooks very quickly. Remove from the oven and run a knife around the rim of the cake, then invert it onto a wire rack. Remove the paper and let cool.

5. MAKE THE BLACKBERRY SYRUP: Place the sugar and water in a small saucepan and stir to dissolve the sugar. Bring to a boil and cook for 2 minutes, until syrupy. Stir in the liqueur and remove from the heat. Let cool to room temperature.

6. MAKE THE MOUSSE: Fill a small bowl with the ice water. Sprinkle the gelatin over the surface and let sit for 5 minutes. Chill the cream inside a stainless bowl along with the beaters for 15 minutes.

7. Meanwhile, process the thawed berries in a food processor or blender to a purée. Pass through a fine sieve to remove the seeds, pressing down to release as much purée as possible. You should have about 1½ cups.
Transfer the purée to a small saucepan and heat slowly with the sugar, whisking until completely dissolved. Bring just to a boil, then add the gelatin and stir until it, too, is dissolved. Remove from the heat and chill quickly by immersing the pot into a bowl containing ice and water. Keep stirring gently until the mixture is a little cooler than room temperature.

8. Whip the cream until thick, then fold in the berry purée. Set aside while you assemble the cake in the springform pan.

9. ASSEMBLE THE CAKE: Clean the springform pan. Snap the rim around the base, then grease the base and sides lightly with butter. Line the pan with 2 large sheets of plastic wrap, crisscrossing them so they cover the bottom and sides. You want the plastic long enough so the flaps can fold over the finished cake. (The butter helps the plastic stick to the sides of the pan.)

10. Measure the ladyfingers by standing one so it just clears the rim of the springform pan. Trim off the top end if you need to with a serrated knife, then cut the remaining ladyfingers so they are all the same size.

11. LAYER THE FILLING: Place the cooled sponge cake back into the pan (on top of the plastic wrap). Prick the cake all over with a toothpick, then brush the surface with half of the blackberry syrup. Brush the remaining syrup lightly across the flat side of each ladyfinger, then tuck them into the perimeter of the pan with the flat sides facing in, wedging them between the cake and the rim of the pan so they stand upright.
Next, pour in blackberry mousse. Pat the side of the pan gently to remove any air bubbles. Loosely fold the plastic wrap over the mousse, and place in the refrigerator for several hours or overnight, until set.

12. When the mousse is firm, gently unhook the springform pan and remove the base. Slide the cake onto a decorative serving dish, using a large spatula and the overhanging plastic wrap to hold the cake together. Lift the edges very gingerly and remove the plastic wrap from underneath the cake.

13. MAKE THE TOPPING: Whip the cream with the liqueur and powdered sugar until thick. Transfer to a pastry bag fitted with a star tip. Pipe lavishly over the top of the cake (or just spoon it on in spiky dollops) and chill until ready to serve.

Snow Queen Treats

For a dancer, the highlight of the holiday season is the opening of the Nutcracker. Each year measures the development of one's career, elevating those most dedicated to more challenging and prestigious roles, from tippy-toed angel and skipping Bon Bon through the ranks in a Darwinian climb to the most coveted parts: the Sugarplum Fairy and her Cavalier. Most dancers determine at an early age their desire to have a career on stage, usually after witnessing their first Nutcracker performance. It might strike as a tingle of inspiration when the prima ballerina enters with her Cavalier to dance the Grand Pas de Deux but for me it was always the Snow Scene. Whether I was backstage or watching from the audience, I loved the shimmering icicles and snow-capped mountains painted on backdrops, the lighting as blue as moonlight, and the tiny glistening flakes of snow that fell from the skies of the theater like powdered sugar being tapped through a sifter. The Snowflakes resembled not a corps of girls spinning to music, but a corps who became the music. The dancers could sauté in circles and turn in patterns as fast as the storm blew around them without ever slipping or straying out of line. I remember feeling such chills of excitement watching my first Nutcracker that it was all I dreamt about for weeks afterwards! Because I also happened to be viewing it from the gods at Lincoln Center, it was unlike many performances I have witnessed since–for all the pleasure of critical scrutiny a more proximal and premium-priced seat may have offered, it couldn't compare to watching the Snow Scene from the highest balcony. From a bird's-eye view, it was all the more captivating, like peering inside a snow globe without having to shake it.

Snow Rose Sorbet 56

Green Tea and Mint Sorbet with Almond Tuiles 58

Chocolate Chip Cookie Ice Cream Sandwiches 60

Gilded Snowball 63

Earl Grey Ice Cream 64

Arabian Coffee and Kahlua Gelato 65

Chestnut Crêpes with Vanilla Bean Ice Cream and Warm Caramel Bananas 67

Bon Bons 69

Champagne Poached Pears with Cardamom Honey Ice Cream and Rich Chocolate Sauce 71

It seems no dessert earns as much applause as ice cream. Dreamy, creamy, cool, and satisfying–there may be nothing more refreshing at the peak of summer, but I know as many people willing to brave any snowstorm just for a single or double scoop of their favorite flavor. When I was growing up, no ballet recital was complete without a celebratory trip afterwards to the local Friendly's for a sundae, and there is still nothing better after a performance than relaxing with a pint of my flavor of the month propped in my lap. When I was dancing in Italy, my dessert of choice was gelato, and since it was both irresistible and ubiquitous, my post-performance treat became a requisite finale to every meal–I considered it a digestive.

As a professional dancer, I spent many of the hottest months of summer performing outdoors, where the temperature on stage would often climb past 100 degrees. On those evenings my ritual ice cream was replaced with icy smooth sorbet. Since I felt commercial brands always tasted too sweet, I bought a machine and experimented with my own flavors, using fresh mint leaves I had grown in a pot on my window sill, or locally grown raspberries or lemons from the farmers market. As I became more adventurous, I played with more unusual ingredients like herbs and spices, and organic tea blends from fancy tea shops. I made small batches and ate them out of the container while icing my feet with bags of frozen vegetables, savoring each spoonful of finely shaved crystals melting on my tongue. Sorbet is still one of my favorite desserts, perfect in any weather, and naturally figure-friendly.

Snow Queen Treats offers frosty fantasies from the creamiest gelatos, ice creams and sorbets to more elaborate frozen desserts. If you don't have an ice cream maker, some of the recipes will be just as delicious substituting store-bought brands.

Snow Rose Sorbet

This flowery sorbet isn't so much a dessert as an entremets, or palate cleanser, flavored with a hint of icy rose and mint. It is gracefully cooling and refreshing and should be served in precious little portions in small fine glasses in between the courses of an elegant meal. It is made from a specially blended tea by the same name that I purchase from the Imperial Tea House in San Francisco, where they combine an intoxicating mixture of rose, mint, and camomile leaves. You can make your own mixture by combining equal amounts of loose dried rose hips, chamomile, and mint tea leaves.

SIMPLE SYRUP

2 cups sugar

1¾ cups water

SORBET

2 cups boiling water

¼ cup Snow Rose tea (about 6 tea bags)

1. PREPARE THE SIMPLE SYRUP: Stir the sugar and water together in a medium-sized pot until the sugar is dissolved. Bring to a boil, then lower the heat and simmer for 10 minutes, until syrupy. Let cool to room temperature.

Extra syrup should be stored in the refrigerator, tightly covered, and can be used for sweetening iced tea and mixed drinks, and as a base for poaching fruits.

2. MAKE THE SORBET: Sprinkle the tea leaves into a small pot and pour the boiling water over them. Let steep for 1 hour, or until the water is fully cooled, then pour through a fine strainer. Pour the infused tea again through cheesecloth to remove any tiny leaves or residual particles. Stir in ¾ cup of the simple syrup until thoroughly combined, then freeze in an ice cream maker or sorbetier according to the manufacturer's instructions.

NOTE

If you don't have an ice cream maker or sorbetier (sorbet maker), the unique flavor of Snow Rose will be highlighted just as well in the form of a crunchy granita. Using an everyday metal tray or casserole (not nonstick), a fork, and a little muscle, you can achieve the granular texture of a snow cone, or freeze it solid and break it with an ice pick into small, pale pink diamonds.

For a granita, pour the sweetened tea into a metal tray and freeze until slushy, then whisk the mixture with a fork to break up the ice particles. Freeze again for another 20 minutes, and whisk again. Repeat freezing and whisking once more if you prefer a smoother texture. Store in a covered plastic freezer container.

Chinese Green Tea and Mint Sorbet
with Almond Tuiles

Unlike green tea ice cream, this cooling sorbet has no musty aftertaste, with a refreshing mint flavor and subtle green tea background. Served with delicate almond cookies for a light and elegant dessert. You can use either Japanese or Chinese green tea, but try to find loose whole leaves, which stay fresher longer than what often ends up crushed into bags. Look for gunpowder, sencha, or lung ching varieties.

GREEN TEA AND MINT SORBET

1 tablespoon loose Chinese green tea leaves

1 tablespoon mint tea leaves

½ cup fresh spearmint leaves

4 cups boiling water

1¼ cups sugar

3 to 4 drops green food coloring

1. Let the green tea, mint tea, and spearmint leaves steep in the boiling water for 5 minutes. Pass through a fine-mesh sieve into another bowl. Stir in the sugar until completely dissolved. Add the food coloring, one drop at a time until you achieve a pale green shade slightly darker than that of the costume at the left. The color will be slightly lighter once the sorbet has frozen. Let cool completely, then freeze until set in an ice cream maker or sorbetier according to the manufacturer's directions.

2. Transfer to a chilled metal pan or baking tin and freeze until firm. Serve with the tuile cookies.

ALMOND TUILES

½ cup (1 stick) unsalted butter, at room temperature

1 cup powdered sugar

¾ cup all-purpose flour, sifted

3 egg whites

½ teaspoon almond extract

1. In a medium bowl, cream the butter until light and fluffy. In a separate bowl, mix the powdered sugar and flour together, then beat into the butter just until combined. Add the egg whites, one at a time, and then the almond extract, mixing until well-blended. Chill the tuile batter for 30 minutes.

2. Preheat the oven to 350°F.

3. On a baking sheet lined with parchment paper, use an offset spatula to spread 2 teaspoons of batter into a small, flat circle, about 3 inches in diameter. Repeat to make 5 or 6 tuiles at a time, so you will have time to bend each tuile before it crisps up. Keep the batter in the fridge in between batches.

4. Bake the tuiles for 4 to 6 minutes, until light brown on the edges. Remove from the oven and immediately lift each tuile with a spatula and lay it over a rolling pin. If you are more ambitious, you can quickly roll them while they are still warm into cigarettes around the round handle of wooden spoon, or just leave them as flat little disks—they will taste just as good. Once they are set, store for up to 1 week in an airtight container.

Chocolate Chip Cookie Ice Cream Sandwiches

I have to include these ice cream sandwiches because I make them every Christmas, varying the flavors of ice cream with different kinds of chocolate. In place of semisweet, try mint- or orange-flavored chocolate, cut into rough chunks, or for a more festive look, use red and green M&M's.

CHOCOLATE CHIP COOKIES

1½ cups all-purpose flour

¾ teaspoon baking soda

¾ teaspoon salt

¾ cup (1½ sticks) unsalted butter, room temperature

¾ cup dark brown sugar

¼ cup granulated sugar

1 whole egg

1 egg yolk

¾ teaspoon vanilla extract

1¼ cups (8 ounces) semisweet chocolate chips, or half semisweet and half white chocolate chips

1 quart of your favorite ice cream, softened

1. Preheat the oven to 350°F. Line 2 baking sheets with parchment paper.

2. MAKE THE COOKIES: In a medium bowl, stir together the flour, baking soda, and salt. In a large bowl, cream the butter and sugars until light and fluffy. Beat in the egg and then the yolk and vanilla extract. Now, with the mixer on the lowest setting, add the flour just until it is incorporated into the batter. I used to know a chocolate chip cookie connoisseur who considered how the flour is added vital enough to the success of the recipe that he would massage the flour into the dough with his fingers—that part is up to you.

3. Stir in the chips, then freeze the dough until it is firm, at least 1 hour—if the dough isn't cold enough, the cookies will spread out too thin as they bake.

4. Scoop out the frozen dough about 3 tablespoons at a time, and drop 2 inches apart on the baking sheets. Bake for 8 to 10 minutes, or until the edges are golden brown. Let rest on the baking sheet for 2 minutes, then transfer to a rack to cool completely. Makes 40 cookies. You'll need only 16 cookies for the ice cream sandwiches.

5. MAKE THE ICE CREAM SANDWICHES: Once you have baked and cooled the chocolate chip cookies, scoop about ½ cup ice cream and sandwich between 2 cookies. Repeat to make 8 ice cream sandwiches. Wrap each sandwich individually in plastic and keep frozen until ready to serve.

Yes, this is a fancy name for an old favorite, but this version of baked Alaska is made seasonally chic with red and white peppermint bits. You can make the ice cream from scratch (*see page 72*) or mix some roughly crushed peppermint candies into softened store-bought ice cream. The cake base and ice cream can be molded and frozen weeks in advance, but once you cover it with the meringue, serve right away.

1 store-bought pound cake (12 ounces), cut into ¾-inch slices

1 quart French vanilla ice cream, softened

½ cup crushed peppermint candies

MERINGUE

4 large egg whites, at room temperature

1 cup sugar

⅛ teaspoon cream of tartar

½ teaspoon vanilla extract

1. PREPARE THE ICE CREAM AND CAKE BASE: For the snowball pictured on the left, I used a wide 7-inch stainless metal bowl, but any shallow 1-quart bowl will work.
Lightly butter or spray the bowl with vegetable oil spray. Take 2 long sheets of plastic wrap and crisscross them to line the interior of the bowl, letting the ends overhang.

2. Line the base of the bowl with the cake slices, reserving 4 slices to fit over the base once the ice cream has been added. Mix the peppermints into the softened ice cream, then transfer to the cake-lined bowl. Spread evenly so the top is flat.

3. Press the reserved cake slices over the ice cream, cutting pieces to fill any gaps so the entire surface is covered. Fold the overhanging plastic wrap back over the cake and place in the freezer until the ice cream is hard, at least 4 hours or up to 2 weeks.

4. When you are ready to serve the snowball, preheat the oven to 450°F or have ready a small kitchen torch (the kind used for making crème brûlée).

5. MAKE THE MERINGUE: Combine the egg whites and sugar in a stainless bowl set over a small pot of barely simmering water. Using a hand-hold electric mixer, beat the egg whites until glossy and stiff, about 10 minutes. Stir in the vanilla. Transfer the meringue to a pastry bag.

6. Remove the bowl of ice cream from the freezer. Turn the bowl over and run warm water over the bottom for a few seconds to loosen the plastic. Invert it onto a baking tray if you will be using the oven or onto a serving dish if you have a kitchen torch.

7. Unwrap the plastic and pipe the meringue in decorative spikes over the dome, covering it completely. Place in the oven just until the meringue begins to brown, or burnish it lightly with the torch. Serve immediately.

Earl Grey Ice Cream

Makes 1 quart

2 cups heavy cream

2 cups whole milk

4 Earl Grey tea bags

6 egg yolks

½ cup sugar

8 ounces white chocolate, chopped

1. INFUSE THE MILK AND CREAM: In a medium pot with a lid, bring the heavy cream and milk to a boil. Add the tea bags and let infuse for 15 minutes, then strain the mixture, squeezing the tea bags to get every bit of flavor out. Discard the bags.

2. TEMPER THE EGG YOLKS: In another bowl set over but not touching simmering water, whip the yolks with the sugar until thick and pale. Pour a little of the infused cream into the whipped yolks and mix well to temper them, then pour the mixture back into the pot containing the remaining cream and stir well.

3. COOK THEN COOL THE CUSTARD: Return the custard to the heat and cook, stirring, over medium-low heat, until cream coats the back of a wooden spoon. Remove from the heat and sprinkle in the chopped white chocolate. Let sit for a few minutes, then steadily whisk until the chocolate is completely melted and the custard is smooth. Place the pot in a large bowl filled with ice and water to quickly bring down the temperature. Transfer to a bowl and chill for several hours or overnight before freezing in an ice cream maker according to the manufacturer's instructions.

This is a very upscale-tasting ice cream, the kind you find these days in tiny scoops in trendy restaurants, yet using tea as a flavoring in desserts was also common back when Hoffmann was busy writing his famous Nutcracker tale. Throughout the 19th century, confections infused with tea were highly fashionable among the privileged classes. While Arabian coffee was prized for its exotic taste and perceived digestive benefits, sweet desserts flavored with tea symbolized good fortune.

This unusual white chocolate ice cream is rich and luxuriously exotic, due to a subtle hint of bergamot, or Cantonese orange oil, which gives Earl Grey its distinctive flavor. The tea also has the benefit of balancing white chocolate's tendency to be overly sweet. The result is a superb partner to dense chocolate cakes or tarts, or just as satisfying served solo in a bowl.

Arabian Coffee and Kahlúa Gelato

1 cup heavy cream

3 cups whole milk

1 cup sugar

¼ cup Kahlúa liqueur

2 tablespoons instant coffee

8 egg yolks

1. Combine the cream, milk, ½ cup of the sugar, and the Kahlúa in a medium saucepan. Bring just to the point of boiling, then remove from the heat. Add the coffee granules and stir until the sugar and coffee are dissolved.

2. Place the egg yolks and remaining ½ cup of sugar in a stainless bowl. Set over a pot of simmering water, or do what I do and prop the bowl right over the pot of the just-boiled cream and milk. Beat until the yolks are thick and lightened, scraping the bowl often to make sure all the sugar is dissolved.
Add a few dollops of the cream to the beaten egg yolks and stir well, then mix in the remaining cream and milk. Place over medium heat and keep stirring until the custard thickens enough to coat the back of a wooden spoon, about 5 minutes. Remove from the heat and pour into a bowl.

3. Chill the custard for several hours or, better yet, overnight, then freeze in an ice cream maker according to the manufacturer's instructions.

This deliciously easy dessert showcases beautiful autumn pears. It can be both elegant or informal, depending on the plates you decide to serve them on. Bartlett pears tend to have more flavor than Bosc pears when they are ripe, although the Boscs' long, graceful stems add a feminine touch to the plated dessert. Either variety tastes wonderful saturated with the sweet champagne syrup. Leaving the stem on also makes them easier to turn while they are poaching.

Champagne Poached Pears with Cardamom and Honey Ice Cream and Rich Chocolate Sauce

POACHED PEARS

1 vanilla bean, split lengthwise

1 cup sugar

3 cups champagne

zest of half a lemon, cut into 2-inch strips

2 tablespoons lemon juice

4 Bosc or Bartlett pears, ripe but still firm

CARDAMOM AND HONEY ICE CREAM

2 cups heavy cream

2 cups whole milk

8 whole cardamom pods

¼ cup sugar

10 large egg yolks

½ cup honey

Rich Chocolate Sauce (see page 142)

1. POACH THE PEARS: Gently scrape out seeds of the vanilla bean and place the seeds and bean in a medium saucepan large enough to hold the pears. Add the sugar, champagne, lemon zest, and lemon juice and place over medium-high heat. Bring this poaching liquid to a boil.

2. Peel and core the pears, leaving the stems on. As soon as the poaching liquid comes to a boil, turn the heat down to low and gently lay the pears in the liquid. Simmer until they are tender but still hold their shape, 20 to 25 minutes, turning them over halfway through the cooking time. Remove pears and place in a shallow bowl to cool.

3. Boil the poaching liquid down until it is syrupy and reduced by 50%. You should end up with about 1½ cups of syrup. Remove from the heat and let cool, then pass through a fine sieve and pour the strained liquid over the cooled pears. Cover the dish loosely with plastic, then chill for several hours or overnight.

4. MAKE THE CARDAMOM AND HONEY ICE CREAM: Combine the heavy cream, milk, cardamom pods and 2 tablespoons of the sugar in a medium saucepan. Bring to a simmer, then turn the heat off. Cover the pan and let the cardamom pods infuse the mixture for 20 minutes. Pour through a fine strainer and discard the cardamom pods. Let cool.

5. While the cream and milk are infusing, combine the egg yolks and remaining 2 tablespoons of sugar in a bowl. Beat with a whisk or electric beaters until the yolks are thick and light lemon in color.

6. Pour the infused cream into the thickened yolks a little at a time, stirring all the while until fully incorporated. Pour this custard into a pot over medium-low heat and cook, stirring with a wooden spoon, for 3 to 4 minutes more, until thickened enough to coat the back of the spoon. Drizzle in the honey and stir for another minute or so, until the honey has melted and disappeared into the custard.

7. Remove from the heat and set the pot into a large bowl of ice and water to cool, then transfer to a bowl and cover loosely with plastic. Refrigerate for several hours or, better yet, overnight.

8. When the custard has thoroughly chilled, transfer to an ice cream maker and freeze according to the manufacturer's instructions.

9. TO SERVE: Slice the pears in half lengthwise and place in shallow bowls. Place a scoop of ice cream on top of one of the pear halves, then serve with chocolate sauce alongside.

Crouching between the folds of Mother Ginger's skirt hides a gaggle of little acrobat children called bon bons. As Mother Ginger reaches the center of the stage, they burst out to surprise the audience, then perform a series of skips and turns while Mother Ginger primps and preens in her mirror. These luscious ice cream bon bons can be both sophisticated and kid-friendly depending on what flavor of ice cream you use. Like most frozen desserts, they are great for entertaining, since they can be made ahead of time and piled into a fancy dessert glass just before it's time to serve.

1 quart vanilla ice cream, softened

8 ounces dark chocolate, chopped

8 ounces white chocolate, chopped

8 ounces milk chocolate, chopped

3 tablespoons vegetable shortening

1. Let the ice cream soften until you are able to scoop it out into 1-inch balls. Make about 2 dozen balls, or as many as you can get out of the quart of ice cream, and place them on a baking tray in the freezer. I find it easier to place each ball in the freezer as I go so they don't melt, especially if it is a warm day.

2. While the ice cream balls are freezing, melt the dark chocolate and 1 tablespoon of the shortening together in a double boiler over low heat. Do the same in separate pots with the white and milk chocolates. Let cool slightly.

3. Working with one ice cream ball at a time, insert a toothpick and dip the ice cream into one of the melted chocolates, coating it completely, then place back in the freezer until set. When the chocolate coating is completely hard, transfer the bon bons to a covered container and freeze until ready to serve.

Chestnut Crêpes with Vanilla Bean Ice Cream and Warm Caramel Bananas

Fine chestnut flour adds a subtle nutty flavor to these delicate crêpes. They are the perfect foil for warm caramelized bananas and homemade vanilla ice cream. To make them extra-special, garnish with slivers of marrons glacés.

CRÊPES

2 eggs

¾ cup milk

½ cup water

½ cup all-purpose flour

½ cup chestnut flour

4 teaspoons sugar

pinch of salt

3 tablespoons unsalted butter, melted

clarified butter or vegetable oil for cooking the crêpes

4 large, ripe bananas

½ cup light brown sugar

½ cup (1 stick) unsalted butter

2 tablespoons rum

1 cup heavy cream

1 quart vanilla ice cream, store-bought or homemade (page 72)

powdered sugar, for dusting, optional

1. PREPARE THE CRÊPES: The easiest way to make the crêpe batter is to whisk all the ingredients together in a bowl or blend them in a blender until smooth. Let rest at room temperature for 30 minutes.

2. When you are ready to cook the crêpes, heat an 8-inch crêpe pan over medium heat. Brush the pan with a little clarified butter or vegetable oil, then pour in ¼ cup of batter. Quickly swirl the batter around by tilting your wrist back and forth so the base of the pan is coated as evenly and thinly as possible.

3. Cook for about 30 seconds, or until the edges turn a dry, light brown. Slide a spatula underneath and flip to the other side. Cook for another 30 seconds or so, just until lightly browned, then slide the crêpe onto a sheet of waxed paper to cool. Don't worry if the first crêpe doesn't come out well—crêpe pans often need one test run before they are properly warmed up.

Store the crêpes at room temperature if you will eat them the same day or freeze, tightly wrapped, for up to 1 month.

4. PREPARE THE BANANAS: Peel the bananas and slice them 1-inch thick. Set aside.

Heat the brown sugar and butter in a large sauté pan over medium heat. Stir until the sugar has melted. Add the rum and cook for 1 minute over medium-high heat. Reduce the heat and add the cream. Let it bubble away for a few seconds, then slowly stir with a whisk until smooth. Stir in the bananas and remove from the heat.

5. TO SERVE: If the crêpes have been chilled or frozen, thaw to room temperature then wrap in foil and rewarm them gently in a low (200°F) oven for 15 minutes. Place a scoop of ice cream onto each crêpe and roll to enclose. Top with a few spoonfuls of the caramel bananas. Shake some powdered sugar over, if you like, and serve straight away.

VANILLA BEAN ICE CREAM

2 cups whole milk

2 cups heavy cream

1 vanilla bean, split lengthwise

1 cup sugar

8 egg yolks

1. Bring the milk and cream to a simmer in a medium pot. Scrape in the seeds from the vanilla bean and add to the cream, along with the scraped bean. Turn the heat off and let infuse for 15 minutes. Discard the bean and set the mixture aside to cool.

2. In a large bowl, beat the sugar with the egg yolks until thick and pale. Add a little of the vanilla cream and mix well, then stir in the remaining cream. Return to medium-low heat and cook, stirring, until the mixture thickens enough to coat the back of a wooden spoon. Remove from the heat and chill completely (overnight for the creamiest texture), then freeze in an ice cream maker according to the manufacturer's instructions. Makes 1 quart.

Crêpe Technique

Successful crêpe making relies on three things: the right temperature pan, having a well-rested batter that pours thinly, and tilting the crêpe pan so the batter coats the base evenly before it begins to set. It isn't difficult, just a matter of getting the rhythm in your wrist.

Crêpe batter is similar to American pancake batter, with a higher liquid content so it can be poured paper-thin. To make the batter, you can whizz the ingredients together in a food processor or blender or whisk them by hand—what is important is to let the batter rest for at least 30 minutes before you use it. The resting time allows the batter to settle and so excess air bubbles will be dispersed, facilitating crêpes that are flat and delicately golden. The finished crêpes should be lightly veined with brown, not burned in spots, and should cook on each side in less than a minute. Place the cooked crêpes on a plate, separating them with paper towels, and store in a warm (200°F) oven until ready to serve. Extras can be wrapped in foil and frozen for up to 1 month.

Whether you use a nonstick or regular pan is up to you; just make sure it is heavy and has no hot spots (parts that cook unevenly). If you are using a cast-iron pan, you can proof it to create a more non-stick surface by filling it with a cup or so of salt and placing it over medium-low heat for 30 minutes. The salt will absorb any moisture or oil. Do not rinse clean, just wipe thoroughly with a paper towel.

Also, doing double duty with two pans instead of one saves a lot of time, so if you like crêpes as much as I do, invest in two good-quality pans in an 8- to 9-inch size—any larger and the crêpes tend to be more difficult to flip and the smaller sizes make crêpes that are too small to be folded—better for making those tiny Russian pancakes called blini.

Petits Divertissements

$\mathcal{T}$he holidays have always been my favorite season. Not only did I get to perform night after night, but it was also an ideal opportunity for my two passions to be deliciously intertwined: I actually got to dance roles that were also my favorite things to eat! On stage and off, from late September until early in the new year, I nibbled on marzipan and dried fruit, candy canes, cookies, and cakes. A cornucopia of homemade candies and chocolate, spiced and sugared nuts wrapped in shiny packages were often exchanged as gifts backstage and provided enough fuel for a sugar high that lasted well through each night's finale. The recipes in this chapter of Petits Divertissements are inspired by all those delectable little goodies I enjoyed during my Nutcracker seasons and all the unforgettable treats I've enjoyed since then: individual-sized cakes and pastries, cookies and bon bons—bite-sized treats to delight your family and friends, from the littlest mice to the king-sized sweet tooth. Enjoy elegant petits fours inspired by the famous French torte Opéra, and dainty little Marzipan Mice, covered in rich milk chocolate. Try Chocolate Candy Canes for an easy way to add a festive touch to holiday parties, or Star Anise Shortbread, Fancy Cookies, and delicate miniature Pavlova for lovely desserts any time of year. Krakatuk Nut Truffles or rich and sophisticated Bittersweet Truffles with Candied Orange Zest make wonderful gifts, as do jazzy Nut Brittle Brigade and Sunflower and Sesame Brittle. Wrapped in shiny cellophane and tied with a bright bow, these little treats are sure to win rave reviews.

Petite Pavlova

The Dying Swan (Le Cygne) was choreographed by Michel Fokine in St. Petersburg in 1905 as a solo for a rising young ballerina with the Maryinsky Theatre named Anna Pavlova. The technically precise yet emotional piece was set to the mournful Swan movement from Saint Saëns' suite *Carnival of the Animals,* presenting the ballerina as a beautiful swan who has just been pierced in the heart by a hunter's arrow. Frail and faltering, the dance shows the young swan struggling toward her last breath. The two-minute solo was arranged in only a few rehearsals, choreographed largely out of patterns of tiny steps on pointe called bourrées, yet despite its simplicity, the piece came to symbolize the emotional power of ballet. In the August 1931 issue of Dance Magazine, Fokine said, "It was like a proof that the dance could and should satisfy not only the eyes, but through the medium of the eye should penetrate into the soul." Pavlova's Dying Swan became her most identifying role, and one against which all subsequent ballerinas' portrayals have been compared.

For holiday parties, I like to make at least one dessert for those who prefer their treats (and their hips!) pint-sized. These little Pavlovas always fit the bill. Miniature puffs of meringue, crowned with a trio of fresh raspberries, kiwi, and pomegranate seeds and topped with a dollop of whipped cream, are light yet luscious. You can make the meringues up to a week ahead and store them in a tightly covered tin, but once assembled with the fruit and cream they will quickly go soft, so dress them at the last minute and serve tout de suite.

When Anna Pavlova toured Australia in 1926 to perform excerpts from The Nutcracker, this light as air dessert was named in her honor because of the way the meringue resembled the layers of tulle in her tutu.

MERINGUES

6 large egg whites, at room temperature

1 teaspoon fresh lemon juice

½ teaspoon vanilla extract

1 cup superfine sugar

1½ tablespoons cornstarch

1 cup heavy cream

2 tablespoons powdered sugar, plus more for dusting

seeds from 1 fresh pomegranate

1 cup fresh raspberries

1 fresh kiwi, peeled, quartered and sliced into small triangles

1. MAKE THE MERINGUES: Preheat the oven to 200°F.

2. Combine the egg whites, lemon juice, and vanilla in a medium bowl. Whip with an electric mixer on medium speed until soft peaks form. Slowly add the sugar and keep beating until you have a stiff and glossy meringue.
Gently sift the cornstarch over the meringue and fold it in with a spatula.

3. Drop little pillows of the meringue (about ½ cup meringue each) 2 inches apart onto a Silpat or waxed paper-lined baking sheet.

4. Bake for about 1½ hours, or until crisp on the outside and and soft like marshmallows on the inside. Transfer to racks to cool.

5. Just before serving, whip the heavy cream with 2 tablespoons powdered sugar until thick. Transfer to a pastry bag and pipe a small dollop atop each pavlova. Adorn the tops with a few jeweled pomegranate seeds, 1 or 2 raspberries, and a quartered slice of kiwi. Dust with powdered sugar and serve immediately.

You might think that the occupants of the Land of the Sweets were a serendipitous cast of characters, inspired by Hoffmann's own confectionary preferences, yet the delicacies chosen to dance their welcome for Marie and the Nutcracker Prince were featured not only for their exquisite taste, but also for the prestige associated with their acquisition. Arabian coffee and sweets, Chinese tea, and the milled sugared almonds that were turned into marzipan figures represented some of the finest foodstuff money could buy during Hoffmann's day. Ingredients that were imported were expensive, so desserts containing exotic spices and flavorings were usually reserved for special occasions.

The flaky nut pastry baklava is one of the most popular of such desserts. This Arabian variation is flavored with cardamom and soaked with rose syrup. Rose water can be purchased in most Middle Eastern grocery stores.

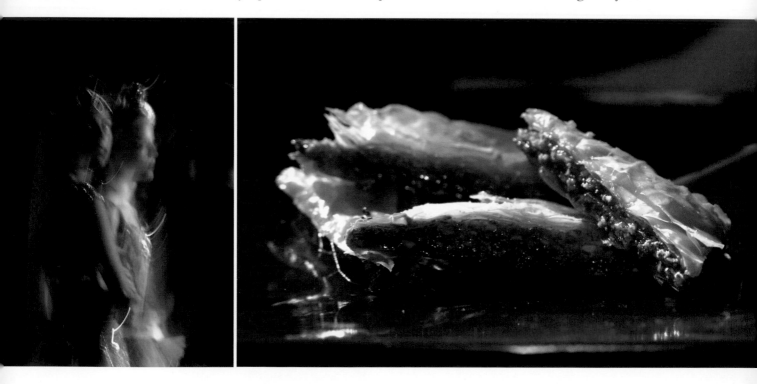

Baklava

1 cup blanched almonds

1 cup shelled pistachios

½ cup sugar

1 teaspoon ground cardamom

12 ounces filo dough (about 18 sheets), at room temperature

2 cups (4 sticks) unsalted butter, melted

ROSE-SCENTED SYRUP

1 cup sugar

1 cup water

2 teaspoons rose water

1. Preheat the oven to 350°F.

2. Combine the nuts, sugar, and cardamom in the bowl of a food processor and pulse until the nuts are finely ground. Set aside.

3. Lightly butter a 12 by 17 by 1-inch baking pan. Unfold the filo dough once it has completely thawed, and lay 1 sheet over the base of the pan. Brush generously with melted clarified butter and top with another sheet of filo. Repeat until you have 6 layers of dough.
Over the base of the filo, spread half of the ground nut mixture. Cover this layer with 6 more sheets of generously buttered filo, then the remaining nuts. Top with 6 more sheets of filo, each brushed again with melted butter. This is a recipe that relies on the butter to stay moist, so don't scrimp: drizzle any that remains over the top.

4. With a very sharp knife, cut the baklava into 40 squares, or slice it diagonally to make diamonds.

5. Bake for 30 minutes, or until the pastry is golden and flaky.

6. PREPARE THE ROSE SYRUP: Combine the sugar and water in a small saucepot. Bring to a boil and cook for about 10 minutes, until thickened. Stir in the rose water. Pour the syrup over the baked baklava and let sit until the layers have absorbed the liquid.

Star Anise Shortbread

Sugar delicately infused with the exotic scent of star anise enhances this simple butter shortbread with holiday spirit. To achieve the lightest crumb, handle the dough as little as possible and chill well before baking.

1½ cups all-purpose flour

½ cup cornstarch

½ cup superfine sugar

2 tablespoons plus ¼ cup star anise sugar (see the opposite page)

¾ cup (1½ sticks) unsalted butter, cut into small pieces

1. Preheat the oven to 325°F.

2. Combine the flour, cornstarch, superfine sugar, and 2 tablespoons of the star anise sugar in a large bowl. Work in the butter using a pastry cutter, 2 knives (one in each hand), or a food processor just until the dough holds together. Gather on a lightly floured surface and squeeze into a ball, then form it into a cylinder or square and slice it any way you like it—I tend to go for irregular triangles for easy dipping in tea.

3. Slice the dough about ¼ inch thick and place on nonstick or lightly greased baking sheets. Sprinkle the tops generously with the remaining ¼ cup of star anise sugar.

4. Place the baking sheets in the refrigerator for 30 minutes, so the dough gets nice and cold and won't spread out when you bake it.

5. Bake for 10 to 12 minutes, just until the edges begin to turn golden. Let cool on racks and store in a tightly covered tin.

Infusing Sugar

Using sugar scented with the heady perfume of fresh herbs, exotic spices, or fragrant vanilla beans makes any dessert extra special. I have so many little jars filled with sugar and various flavorings that my spice chest is beginning to look more like my makeup drawer, but infusing sugar is so easy and the subtle enhancement of flavor it imparts makes even the most mundane recipes enticing. Try a hint of intensely piney fresh rosemary in a fresh-baked pear tart or Tahitian vanilla sugar spooned into fresh-brewed coffee—even the simplest teatime shortbread can be made more exotic by the addition of some star anise-scented crystals. With just a little effort, your desserts can take on a new dimension.

To infuse your sugar, simply toss a bit of spice or fragrant herb into a sugar jar and close it. How strong an infusion you will achieve depends on the amount and freshness of your herb or spice of choice, the length of time it is infused, as well as the proportion of sugar. Rather than exact amounts, think of 1 vanilla bean, 2 to 3 sprigs of fresh herbs, or a spoonful of whole spice per 4 cups of sugar. The general rule is to stick to spices that are large enough to be separated easily when scooping the sugar for use. The exception is cinnamon sugar, which I find never has enough kick when made with whole sticks, so I mix in 1 teaspoon ground cinnamon per cup of sugar—it's great for dressing up French toast, baked sweet potatoes, and fruit pies.

FOR VANILLA SUGAR: Fill clean mason jars halfway with ordinary granulated sugar, then drop in a split vanilla bean (this can be a pod you have scraped of beans already). Cover with more sugar to the top of the jar. After a few days or a few months, use the sugar as you would ordinary sugar, leaving the vanilla bean in the jar and refilling as necessary. You will find that eventually the scent will lose its strength, so discard the used bean after about four months, although I admit I often leave the old beans in for up to six months with no harm done.

Try making fragrant sugar also with star anise, sprigs of fresh rosemary (good for pear and apple tarts), dried lemon and orange zest for stirring into hot tea, or whole cardamom pods (wonderful in rice puddings and Scandinavian pastries). Just a spoonful of fragrant sugar can transform the ordinary into something truly memorable.

Little Cranberry Curd Cookies

TEA COOKIES

1 cup (2 sticks) unsalted butter, at room temperature

1 cup powdered sugar, plus more for dusting

1 egg yolk

1 teaspoon vanilla extract

2¼ cups all-purpose flour

½ teaspoon baking powder

pinch of salt

CRANBERRY CURD

1 package (12 ounces) fresh cranberries

⅔ cup water

juice of 1 lemon

2 teaspoons cornstarch

1 cup sugar

4 egg yolks

6 tablespoons unsalted butter

1. PREPARE THE TEA COOKIES: In a large bowl, beat the softened butter in a mixer for 10 minutes until light and fluffy. Mix in the powdered sugar, egg yolk, and vanilla.
Sift the flour with the baking powder and salt, then stir into the dough in 2 additions, mixing just until incorporated.

2. Place the bowl of dough in the refrigerator and chill for 30 minutes.

3. Preheat the oven to 325°F. Scoop out teaspoonfuls of the chilled dough by and roll between your palms into balls. Space the balls 1 inch apart on an ungreased baking sheet, then flatten with the back of a spatula into rounds.

4. Bake for 10 to 12 minutes, or just until the edges turn light brown. Transfer to a wire rack and dust generously with powdered sugar. Store without filling in an airtight tin for up to 1 week. You should have about 100 cookies.

5. MAKE THE CRANBERRY CURD: The cranberry curd needs to chill thoroughly before using, so make it a day or two in advance. Bring the cranberries to a boil in a medium saucepan over medium heat, along with the water, lemon juice, cornstarch, and sugar. Cook for 5 minutes or so, stirring and mashing until pulpy and all the berries have popped. If necessary, add a tablespoon or two more of water.

6. Remove from the heat and press the mixture through a coarse sieve, so you have a smooth purée.

7. Let cool slightly, then pour the purée back into the pot and beat in the egg yolks. Cook over medium-low heat for another 3 or 4 minutes, until the curd thickens a bit (but don't let it boil). Remove from the heat and pour into a bowl. Whisk in the butter, 1 tablespoon at a time, until smooth. Cover with plastic, pressing right down on the surface to prevent a skin from forming, and let cool completely.

8. TO ASSEMBLE THE COOKIES: Spread 1 teaspoon of the cranberry curd each onto one half of the cookies. Top with the remaining cookies. Shake more powdered sugar through a sifter over the tops. Store the filled cookies in the refrigerator until ready to serve.

With their vibrant ruby color and snowy dusting of powdered sugar, these miniature cranberry curd-filled biscuits are the perfect addition to your Christmas cookie selection. I use a 1¼-inch circular cookie cutter to make them look like large buttons, although you can cut any size or shape you like. The cookies can be stored in an airtight container for up to 1 week, but once filled with the curd, they should be kept refrigerated and will last for up to 3 days. The extra cranberry curd is also delicious spread over fresh scones.

Fancy Cookies

SOUR CREAM PASTRY

2 cups all-purpose flour, sifted

1 cup (2 sticks) unsalted butter, at room temperature

½ cup sour cream

DRIED APRICOT AND PECAN FILLING

½ cup thick apricot preserves

1 cup dried apricots, chopped

2 cups chopped pecans

¼ cup milk

½ cup sugar

2 tablespoons unsalted butter

½ cup powdered sugar

I call these easy little cookies "fancy" because that is what my grandmother called them, despite the fact that they are really just a fortuitous way to use up leftover scraps of pie dough. The dough is one of my favorites: the sour cream makes it soft and supple and it takes less than a minute to make in a food processor. Filled with a thick apricot and pecan filling and baked to flaky perfection, they are similar to Russian rugelach, only more delicate in texture. Eaten warm from the oven, they taste better than anything you can buy in a bakery. My grandma used to vary the fillings to suit whatever was on hand: if no nuts were available, she would spoon dark, thick prune butter, fig preserves, or any chunky jam onto the pastry instead. I invite you to do the same.

1. PREPARE THE SOUR CREAM PASTRY: In a medium bowl, cut the butter into the sifted flour until the mixture resembles coarse crumbs. Work the sour cream in with your hands until you have a soft, pliable pie dough (or pulse in a food processor just until the mixture holds together). The sour cream makes the dough very rich and quite soft, so wrap it in plastic and give it a good chill before you roll it out, at least 30 minutes.

2. While the dough is chilling, prepare the filling by combining the preserves, dried apricots, pecans, milk, sugar, and butter in a pot placed over medium-low heat. Cook, stirring, just until the butter and preserves have melted and the mixture is thick, about 5 minutes. Let cool.

3. Once the dough has chilled for at least 30 minutes, out about ¼ inch thick on a liberally floured surface. Cut into 2-inch squares. Spoon a teaspoon of the filling onto the center of each square, then fold over 2 diagonal corners of each square and pinch together so the filling is encased. Transfer the cookies to an ungreased baking sheet.

4. Bake for 12 to 15 minutes, or just until the edges turn golden. Cool on racks. Before serving, shake powdered sugar generously over the tops.

Marzipan Mice

For several weeks in early December, it has been tradition since long before Hoffmann's day for many German towns to hold a Weinachtsmarkt, or Christmas market. Craftsmen and artisans set up festively decorated booths in the town squares, where they sell hand-carved wooden nutcrackers, artwork, and gifts, along with chocolates, cakes, and hot sausages.

When I was living in Hamburg, I loved to stroll through the aisles of the market, marveling at how magical it all appeared with the colored lights decorating each booth and the aroma of gluhwein and roasting sausages hanging heavy in the air. When the snow began to fall, it was like a scene out of a storybook.

I usually spent most of my time near the confections. Iced gingerbread and lebkuchen came in every shape and size imaginable, but as an American with an addiction to Ritter bars and anything by Niederegger, I found the chocolate and marzipan to be the most enticing. I couldn't resist buying as much as I could carry, with every intention of giving them away as gifts, but my shopping bag was always lighter by the time I got home.

These little mice made from ready-made marzipan are great for making with kids since they require no baking. Buy the extra-fine kind of marzipan if you can find it (I buy mine at a world market), as it is usually a bit softer than the Danish brands found in the grocery store. Otherwise, microwave regular prepared marzipan, wrapped in plastic, on low power until soft enough to mold.

5.3 ounces extra-fine prepared marzipan

8 ounces fine quality milk chocolate, broken into small pieces

sliced almonds, for mice ears

1 ounce dark or white chocolate, for the eyes

1. Divide the marzipan into 10 pieces. Roll each piece between your palms into a ball, then squeeze one end into a teardrop shape with a pointed end.

2. Make 2 slits for the almond ears with the tip of a knife about ½ inch behind the nose of each mouse. Insert a slice of almond into each slit to form ears.

3. Melt half the milk chocolate very gently in a double boiler over simmering water (*see tempering chocolate on page 91*), then stir in the remaining milk chocolate until it is completely melted. If you find there are little grainy bits, press the melted chocolate through a fine sieve and stir again.

4. Cover each mouse with chocolate by inserting a toothpick into the hind end and gently dipping into the chocolate. Coat completely, being careful not to break the almond ears, then gently shake off the excess chocolate by tapping the mouse against the side of a spoon. Transfer to a sheet of parchment paper or Silpat placed on a tray. Repeat for all the mice, then chill until the chocolate is set.

5. To make the eyes, nose, and tail, melt the dark or white chocolate and pour into a pastry bag with a small, plain tip. Make small dots for the eyes and nose, and draw a swirl for the tail. Return to the refrigerator to set.

White Chocolate Macaroons

Be sure to use heavy baking sheets to prevent burning the bottoms of these French-style almond macaroons. If you like, you can substitute dark chocolate in the filling instead of white.

MACAROONS

1⅔ cups toasted unsalted almonds

1 cup superfine sugar

4 large egg whites

2 teaspoons vanilla extract

FILLING

2 ounces white chocolate

2 tablespoons heavy cream

1. MAKE THE MACAROONS: Preheat the oven to 275°F. Line 2 baking sheets with silpat or parchment paper.

2. Pulse the almonds and half of the sugar in a food processor until the nuts are finely ground. (If you don't have superfine sugar, just process regular granulated sugar for a few minutes before adding the almonds.)

3. In a clean, dry bowl, whip the egg whites until you have soft, opaque peaks. Slowly add the remaining ½ cup of sugar and keep beating until very stiff and glossy. Fold in the ground almonds.

4. Spoon the batter by heaping teaspoonfuls onto the prepared sheets and bake for 7 to 10 minutes, until they just begin to brown around the edges. Use a spatula to transfer them to racks.

5. MAKE THE FILLING: Combine the white chocolate and cream in a small saucepan. Set over very low heat until the chocolate is melted. Stir until smooth. Let cool.

6. Make sandwiches by spreading the cooled filling onto half of the macaroons and pressing the remaining macaroons onto them. Store in an airtight container.

Iced Gingerbread Cookies

These crisp cookies are great for gift-giving. To make them into Christmas tree decorations, use a plastic straw to cut holes in the tip of each cookie and be sure to chill the dough well so the holes don't close over as they bake.

COOKIES

3 cups all-purpose flour

1 tablespoon unsweetened cocoa powder

¼ teaspoon salt

½ teaspoon baking soda

1 tablespoon ground ginger

2 teaspoons ground cinnamon

¼ teaspoon ground nutmeg

½ teaspoon ground cloves

½ teaspoon ground cardamom

½ cup (1 stick) unsalted butter, at room temperature

½ cup dark brown sugar

¼ cup sugar

1 egg

½ cup unsulfured molasses

ROYAL ICING

1 pound powdered sugar, sifted

3 egg whites

¼ teaspoon water

1. MAKE THE COOKIE DOUGH: Sift the flour with the cocoa powder, salt, baking soda, and spices. Set aside.

2. In a medium bowl, cream the butter and sugars until light. Beat in the egg and molasses, then slowly add the flour and mix just until incorporated.

3. Scoop the dough onto a large piece of lightly floured waxed paper. Top with another sheet of paper and use a rolling pin to flatten the dough to about ¼ inch thick. Wrap the edges of the paper under and chill the dough for at least 1 hour, until firm.

4. Preheat the oven to 350°F.

5. CUT THE DOUGH: Remove one of the sheets of waxed paper and cut out cookies with a 2-inch metal ring or cookie cutters. Using a spatula, transfer the cookies to a parchment-lined or lightly greased cookie sheet.

6. Bake for 7 to 10 minutes for small cookies or 10 to 12 minutes for larger shapes, until the edges are lightly browned. Let cool on racks completely before decorating with royal icing.

7. MAKE THE ROYAL ICING: Sift the powdered sugar into a medium-sized bowl. Stir in the egg whites and water until the sugar is moistened, then beat until thick and opaque. Transfer to a pastry bag and use immediately to decorate the top of each cookie. Place the decorated cookies back on the rack until the icing has set.

Warming Up Chocolate

Though it may be a stretch to say that chocolate and dancers have a lot in common, they do share some notable qualities. Not only are they tools of unlimited artistic expression, but both can be quite finicky and must be properly conditioned if they are to perform well. Like the muscles and bones, energy and passion that are uniquely coordinated to create great dance, good chocolate is the product of many carefully orchestrated steps.

A wide choice of eating chocolates are available today, from sweet, creamy white and milk varieties to the stark bitter and black varieties favored by chocolate connoisseurs. The potential for chocolate pleasure is unlimited–melted into candies, cakes, cookies, puddings, syrups, or sauces, hot drinks, or mousses, chocolate can be used to flavor, coat, fill, and decorate. The chocolate called for in many of the recipes in this book will simply need to be chopped or melted. In certain types of desserts, however, how chocolate is prepared is very important. If you are making candies or decorations, like the coating for the Krakatuk Nut Truffles or the bark base for the Chocolate Candy Canes, the process of tempering will greatly improve both the taste and appearance of the finished product. Think of the most gratifying and sensual aspects of nibbling a creamy morsel of good-quality chocolate: the glossy shine and crisp snap you hear when you break a piece in two–this is a result of the process of tempering.

Melting Chocolate

The most common method of melting chocolate is in a double boiler, but an equally effective method is in a microwave oven. If I don't feel like washing pots, I will opt for the microwave, although it requires a bit of stop and go to check the progress of the chocolate. Whichever method you choose, always use the lowest heat or power level possible, just until almost melted, then stir until smooth. This helps prevent the chocolate from getting too hot, which can cause it to seize up into a stubborn, lumpy, useless mass. If you are very ambitious, reckless, or very pressed for time, you could melt the chocolate directly over medium heat and stir it constantly until almost melted, then transfer it to a bowl and keep mixing until smooth, but you'll be asking for trouble if you don't keep your eye on it.

1. **Microwave:** This method is economical because it uses only one bowl, but it takes a bit of trial and error until you are familiar with how much power your microwave emits at each setting. Break the chocolate up into small chunks, and place it in a microwave-safe bowl. Microwave at a low setting (usually about 20 percent power) for 30 seconds at a time, stirring after each increment until melted and smooth.

2. **Double boiler:** This category can be subdivided into what I call the stirring and the sweating methods. If you don't have a double boiler, place a bowl over a pot of barely simmering water shallow enough so that the water doesn't touch the bottom of the pot. Break the chocolate up into small chunks, and gently stir until it is almost smooth, then remove the bowl from its steam bath and stir until smooth. Stirring chocolate over a double boiler of softly simmering water is probably the most foolproof method, since you can easily judge when it is time to take the chocolate off the heat.

Sweating the chocolate works well when you are making sauces or icings like white chocolate crème anglaise or dark chocolate ganache, where the recipe calls for hot milk or rich cream to be mixed in with the melted chocolate. Instead of melting the chocolate and heating the liquid separately, you can do it all in one pot. This technique doesn't demand much attention once the chocolate is added and there is no chance of the chocolate seizing on you. Heat your milk or cream to a gentle simmer, then remove it from the heat. Break the chocolate up into small pieces and add it to the pot. Cover it tightly with the lid or a piece of plastic wrap and let stand for 10 minutes. Remove the cover and stir gently until the chocolate is fully incorporated and the mixture is smooth.

White chocolate: If you haven't heard by now, this creamy white confection is not really chocolate at all, but a mixture of cocoa butter, milk, sugar, and vanilla flavoring. Some chocolate die-hards might dismiss white chocolate as ersatz, since it contains no actual cocoa liqueur, but its versatility for decorative purposes and creamy taste has led to a wide assortment of high-quality brands. Valrhona has an exceptionally buttery flavor and is great for cakes, mousses, and puddings, while Lindt brand is slightly less sweet and is milkier tasting, good for making candies or decorative garnishes. Keep any leftover bits tightly wrapped in the fridge for melting into chocolate fondues or dessert sauces, dipping dried fruits, and of course late-night nibbling. Due to its higher cocoa butterfat content, melt white chocolate at a slightly lower temperature than milk or dark chocolate, about 110° to 115° F.

Tempering Chocolate

The shiny gloss and crisp crack of well-tempered chocolate comes from evenly distributed butterfat molecules. You can tell if chocolate is well tempered by breaking a piece in two. You should hear a pleasant snap and the severed edge should be smooth. When preparing chocolate to make candy or decorations, you should melt and cool it properly to keep it from becoming streaky or dull on the surface. Because of its crystalline structure, when chocolate is melted or taken out of "temper," the tiny molecules of cocoa butter need to be brought back to the right temperature to return to a hard, glossy state. This is especially important when you're making molded candies—unlike those in ordinary melted chocolate, the butterfat molecules in tempered chocolate will contract as they cool, so chocolates will pop out of the molds easily once they are set.

To temper milk or dark chocolate, first chop it roughly into little chunks or shards, then melt about two thirds of it in a double boiler over simmering water (don't let the base of the double boiler touch the water). Stir until smooth and test it with a candy thermometer: it should register about 113° to 118°F (dark chocolate may melt at a slightly higher temperature). Add the remaining chocolate, a bit at a time, stirring until all the chocolate is completely melted and the temperature has reduced to 80°F. Place the bowl back over the double boiler for a minute or two to raise the temperature back up to between 84 and 86°F. Use promptly.

Note: Larger amounts of chocolate (1 pound or more) tend to be easier to work with.

Krakatuk Nut Truffles

In *The Story of the Hard Nut*, only a young boy who had neither shaved nor worn boots could break the curse on Princess Pirlipat, by cracking the hardest kernel of all, the Krakatuk nut.

In Hoffmann's day, wooden nut-cracking dolls were popular gifts for children. Holiday trees were often decorated with gold-painted nuts, so the dolls made festive and fitting tools to break open their shells.

Unlike the famous Krakatuk, these milky, rich truffles will melt in your mouth. Made from creamy milk chocolate, they contain a light crunch that comes from finely chopped hazelnuts and caramel, pulsed in a food processor into rough, crackly nuggets.

NUT CRACKLE

½ cup sugar

3 tablespoons water

3 tablespoons chopped toasted hazelnuts

TRUFFLE MIXTURE

6 tablespoons heavy cream

3 tablespoons Frangelico liqueur

8 ounces excellent quality milk chocolate, broken into small pieces

2 tablespoons unsalted butter, cut into small chunks

CHOCOLATE COATING

1 pound excellent-quality milk chocolate

1. PREPARE THE NUT CRACKLE: Boil the sugar and water together until the sugar turns light amber in color, then stir in the nuts and quickly pour onto a well-greased or Silpat-lined baking tray. Cool until hard.

2. Break up the caramel and nuts into large shards, then transfer to a food processor and pulse to grind until the crackle is about the size of large instant coffee granules. Set aside.

3. MAKE THE TRUFFLE MIXTURE: Heat the heavy cream and Frangelico to a simmer, then take off the heat and add the milk chocolate pieces. Let stand for a few minutes, then stir with a whisk until the chocolate is fully incorporated. Drop in the chunks of butter, then whisk again until the mixture is satiny smooth. Let cool to room temperature, then stir in the nut crackle. Cover with plastic and freeze for several hours or chill overnight until firm enough to scoop into balls.

4. When the truffle mixture is firm, scoop and roll it between your palms into teaspoon or tablespoon-sized balls (depending on whether you want small or large truffles). Place on a nonstick or Silpat-lined tray, then chill again if the heat from your hands has made the chocolate soft.

5. MAKE THE CHOCOLATE COATING: Melt the remaining chocolate over barely simmering water until almost melted, then stir until smooth. (For best results you should temper the chocolate, but if the truffles are refrigerated and will be consumed within a day or two, you can just melt the chocolate very carefully over the very lowest heat.)

6. DIP THE TRUFFLES: Toss a few of the truffles into the melted chocolate at a time, pushing them around with the edge of a spoon. Coat each ball completely (keep the remaining truffles in the refrigerator until ready to use).

7. Carefully place the coated truffles back on the tray, then return to the refrigerator until set.
They will last for several days, tightly wrapped, in the refrigerator, but can also be frozen, for up to 1 month.

Noah

Bittersweet Truffles with Candied Orange Zest

TRUFFLE MIXTURE

1½ cups heavy cream

1 pound bittersweet chocolate, finely chopped

¼ cup Grand Marnier or Cointreau liqueur

1 cup finely minced candied orange zest (recipe at right)

¼ cup unsweetened cocoa powder

1 tablespoon powdered sugar

1. PREPARE THE TRUFFLE MIXTURE: In a medium saucepan, bring the cream just to a boil, then remove from the heat. Add the chocolate and orange liqueur. Stir until smooth, then add the candied orange zest. Mix well.

2. Spread the mixture in an 8-inch square nonstick pan and cover with plastic wrap. Let cool to room temperature, then chill for several hours.

3. When the truffle mixture is firm, cut it into ¾-inch squares. Carefully lift out each square with a small spatula. I like them sort of squarish, but you can roll them into balls if you like—just make them small, since they are quite rich.

4. COAT THE TRUFFLES WITH COCOA POWDER: Mix the cocoa powder with the powdered sugar, then pat each truffle with the powder to coat.
Store, tightly wrapped, in the refrigerator for up to 2 weeks or freeze up to 2 months. Bring to room temperature before serving.

CANDIED ORANGE ZEST

1 large navel orange

1 cup sugar

1 to 2 tablespoons water

¼ cup superfine sugar

1. ZEST THE ORANGE: Cut off the top and bottom of the orange, then slide the knife down the sides to cut off the zest in strips (just the outer orange part). Slice each strip into a fine juilienne (very thin strips), about ⅛ inch wide, each. (There is a little kitchen tool called a stripper that is good for this job.)

2. SOFTEN AND REMOVE THE BITTERNESS FROM THE ZEST: Place the strips in a small pot and cover with cold water. Bring to a boil and cook for 5 minutes, then drain the water and replace with fresh cold water. Bring this water to a boil and cook for another 5 minutes, then drain again.

3. Cover the softened orange zest with the sugar. Place over medium-low heat, and add a little water to help the sugar dissolve. Raise the heat and bring the sugar to a boil, then reduce the heat to very low and cook for 15 minutes.

4. DRY THE ZEST: Remove the strips of zest with a fork and spread them out across the bottom of an upturned sieve to drain. Discard the cooking liquid.

5. Place the superfine sugar in a plastic bag and add the orange zest. Shake to coat, then spread on a tray to dry completely. Finely mince the zest before adding it to the truffle mixture.

Chocolate Candy Canes

In Balanchine's Nutcracker, the traditional Russian Trepak variation is replaced by a team of Candy Canes, shaking large hula hoops adorned with jingle bells while the lead male performs an exciting series of acrobatic leaps across the stage.

This chocolate candy cane bark is a fun twist on the usual after-dinner mint. I like to serve it broken into pieces on a silver candy plate, to nibble with coffee. Besides being a festive treat for the holidays, it's a great way to make use of the broken bits at the end of the bag!

7 ounces excellent quality dark chocolate

3 ounces candy canes or red and white peppermints

1. Place the candy canes in a plastic bag and pound lightly with a meat mallet or the bottom of a frying pan into small pieces. You don't want peppermint powder, just broken bits large enough that the red and white stripes are still visible but small enough to provide an equal balance of mint and chocolate with each bite.

2. Melt the chocolate over extremely low heat (so the temperature never rises above 92°F), or temper it according to the directions on page 91. Spread the melted chocolate thinly, about 1/8 inch thick, onto a baking sheet lined with parchment paper or Silpat. The edges don't need to be even, just a freeform puddle of chocolate.

3. Sprinkle the candy cane bits over the surface. Refrigerate until set. Serve broken into pieces.

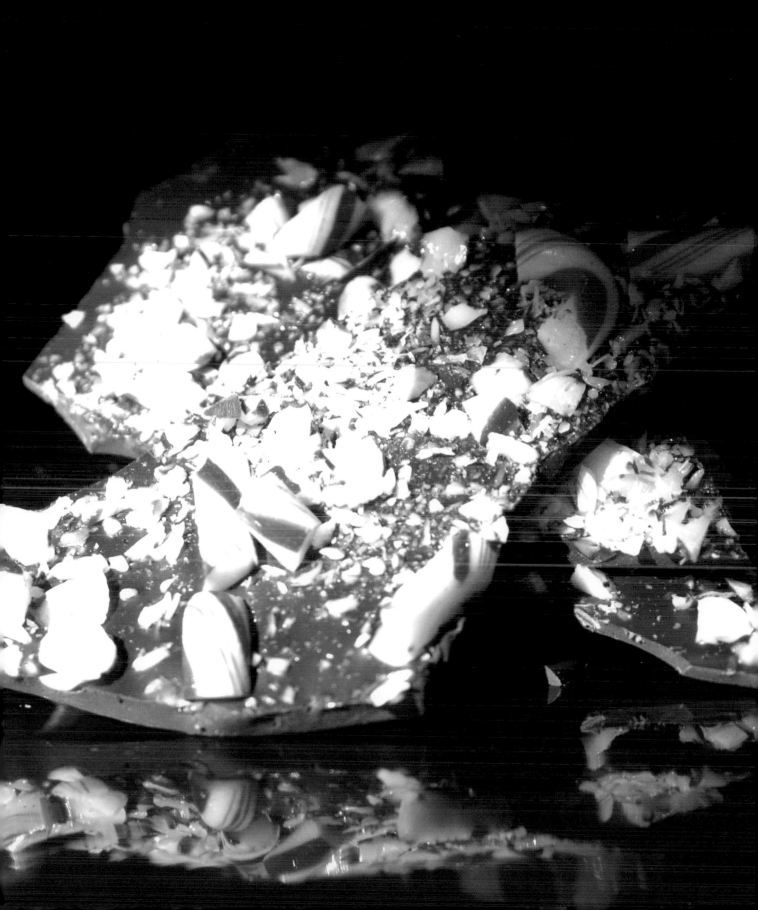

Sunflower Seed and Sesame Brittle

1¼ cups sugar

½ cup water

¼ teaspoon baking soda

½ cup sunflower seeds

¾ cup toasted sesame seeds

1. If you don't have a sheet of Silpat, prepare a baking tray by heavily greasing it with butter.

2. MAKE THE CARAMEL: Combine the sugar and water in a heavy saucepot. Place over medium heat and stir until the sugar dissolves.

3. Raise the heat and boil until the sugar turns amber brown, swirling the pan around if you notice the sugar browning unevenly.

4. Stir in the baking soda and seeds, then quickly pour onto the Silpat or greased tray. Flatten with a greased spatula to ¼ inch thick. Let cool until hard, then crack into pieces. Store in a tightly covered tin.

The sultry Arabian Dance evokes the exotic flavors used in Middle Eastern desserts. This crunchy brittle is filled with sesame and healthy sunflower seeds for a sweet and protein-filled treat.

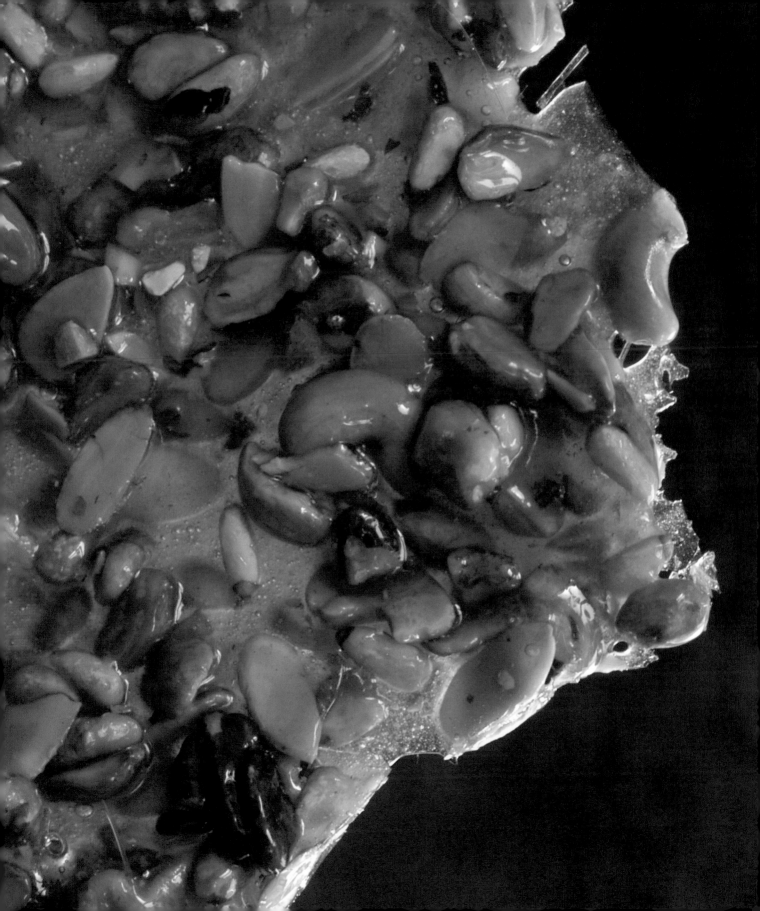

Nut Brittle Brigade

In the 1940s, Duke Ellington rearranged Tchaikovsky's classic Nutcracker score into a sophisticated jazz suite. The Harlem Nutcracker gave the holiday favorite a lively new flavor, complete with vaudevillesque titles for the variations. Sugar Rum Cherry replaced the Dance of the Sugarplum Fairy, and Arabesque Cookie stepped in for Arabian Coffee. This recipe honors the Peanut Brittle Brigade, offering a chorus of different nuts in each bite. Crunchy nut brittle is easy and quick to make and great for gift-giving.

1½ cups unsalted mixed nuts (any combination of walnuts, pine nuts, pistachios, cashews, hazelnuts, almonds, pecans, and/or peanuts)

1 ¼ cups sugar

½ cup water

¼ cup corn syrup

¼ teaspoon baking soda

¼ teaspoon salt

1. Preheat the oven to 350°F. Toast the nuts on a baking sheet until light brown and fragrant. Let cool. Pour the nuts into a bowl, then set aside while you boil the caramel.

2. Combine the sugar, water, and corn syrup in a medium pot and bring to a boil. Once the sugar begins to color, you will need to perform the final steps very quickly, so grease a baking sheet and a spatula heavily with butter and have the baking soda, salt, and nuts measured and ready to add.

3. As soon as the sugar reaches a rich, golden brown, remove the pot from the heat and whisk in the baking soda and salt. Add the nuts all at once, then quickly spread the mixture out onto the baking sheet. Flatten the brittle down to about ¼ inch thick with the buttered spatula, then cool completely until hard.

4. Break the nut pebbled brittle into rough shards and wrap in shiny paper, or pulverize in a food processor to sprinkle over ice cream, puddings, or yogurt.

Petits Rats de L'Opéra

GOLDEN CAKE BASE

1 cup (2 sticks) unsalted butter,
at room temperature

1 cup sugar

4 eggs, lightly beaten

½ teaspoon vanilla extract

1½ cups all-purpose flour

½ teaspoon baking powder

½ cup milk

CHOCOLATE GANACHE

1 cup heavy cream

2 tablespoons unsalted butter

2 tablespoons sugar

6 ounces white chocolate

5 ounces semi-sweet chocolate

COFFEE BUTTERCREAM

2 egg yolks

1 egg

½ cup sugar

1 teaspoon instant coffee

1 tablespoon milk

¾ cup (1½ sticks) unsalted butter, at room temperature

2 (4.41 ounces/125 grams each) boxes Lindt Swiss Thins Chocolates,
one dark and one milk chocolate

¼ cup flaked almonds or slivered pistachios for decorating

My favorite French bakery cake is the decadent and dazzling chocolate and coffee buttercream-layered Opéra, named eponymously after the spectacular belle époque theater in Paris, home of the celebrated French ballet company and where it is said a star ballerina, or étoile, was once entitled to keep her dressing room for life. These miniature renditions of the classic torte are named after the young students, teasingly referred to as the "little rats," at the Opéra training school. Neat and professional little petits fours are inspired by their famous Parisian counterpart, but simplified for home baking by my secret ingredient: Lindt Swiss Thins chocolate squares. Layers of rich, golden vanilla-scented cake are baked extra-thin in a jelly roll pan, then spread with rich chocolate ganache and coffee buttercream filling. The delicate chocolate wafers are placed on top and chilled, then sliced cleanly into perfect little squares.

Foyer of the Palais Garnier, home of
the Paris Opéra Ballet, Paris, France

1. PREPARE THE GOLDEN CAKE: Preheat the oven to 350°F. In a large bowl, cream the butter and sugar together until light and fluffy. Whisk the eggs and vanilla together, then beat into the butter.

2. Sift the flour and baking powder together, then mix into the butter mixture alternately with the milk until you have a smooth, spreadable batter.

3. Grease a large jelly roll pan (11 by 16 inches). Line with parchment paper (or Silpat). Spread 1½ cups of the batter out in a large rectangle, about ¼ inch thick. The idea here is to make an even layer, not achieve the exact pan size, so feel free to use an 11 by 18 inch pan or even a large cookie sheet.

4. Bake for 8 to 10 minutes, watching carefully, until the cake is light golden and springy. Don't worry if the edges brown a little; they will be trimmed away. Flip gently onto a rack and peel off the paper or Silpat.

5. While the first cake is cooling, prepare and bake another layer with an additional 1½ cups of batter. Repeat once more with your remaining batter, spreading to the same thickness. You will not have enough batter to cover the entire sheet, so just spread it to the same thickness as the other layers in as large a square as the batter will allow. You should end up with 2 large rectangles and 1 squarish piece. Let the cakes cool completely.

6. PREPARE THE CHOCOLATE GANACHE: Break the white and semi-sweet chocolate into small pieces. Combine the cream, butter, and sugar in a medium saucepan and place over medium heat. Stir just until the butter is melted and the sugar has dissolved. Remove from the heat and add the chocolate. Cover the pan and let it stand for 5 minutes, then stir gently until the chocolate is melted and the ganache is smooth. Let cool to room temperature.

7. ASSEMBLE THE LAYERS: Lay one layer of the sponge cake on a cutting board and spread some of the cooled chocolate ganache over the surface evenly and completely, about ¼ inch thick. Top with the second layer of sponge cake. Place the whole board in the refrigerator and chill 15 minutes until the ganache is firm. Do the same on the smaller square of cake, but only cover half of the cake with the ganache. (The other half will be covered with the buttercream.)

8. MEANWHILE, PREPARE THE COFFEE BUTTERCREAM: Place the yolks, whole egg, and sugar in a double boiler over simmering water. Stir to dissolve the sugar (until the mixture reaches 110°F, then beat until light and thick. Remove from the heat.

9. Heat the milk in a small saucepan and stir in the coffee until dissolved. Let cool.
In a medium bowl, cream the butter until light and fluffy. Gradually beat in the egg mixture and then the coffee until shiny, thick, and smooth.

10. Once the chocolate ganache layer has set, top with a layer of coffee buttercream, again about ¼ inch thick. Reserve about ¼ cup of buttercream for decorating the tops of each petit four.

11. Gently lay Lindt the chocolate squares over the butter-cream, leaving a ½-inch margin around the edges. Avoid any browned edges of cake, since you will be trimming that part away.
Line the chocolates in a single layer right up next to each other so the entire surface is covered. Try not to leave a margin in between the chocolates—the buttercream will seep out and make them more difficult to cut. Press down with your fingertip ever so gently onto each square to remove any excess air.

12. Cut the remaining layer of cake in half so you have 2 even sized pieces and assemble as just described

13. DECORATE THE TOP OF EACH SQUARE: Place the remaining buttercream into a pastry bag fitted with a small star tip and pipe a swirl onto the center of each chocolate. Top with a slice of flaked almond or a sliver of pistachio. Chill until the buttercream is firm.

14. CUT INTO INDIVIDUAL SQUARES: Using a sharp knife, cut the chilled cake firmly along the edges of the chocolates (I use a thin fillet knife, which fits easily between the squares of chocolate). Dip the knife in hot water and wipe clean with a damp cloth after each cut, so the ganache doesn't smudge the sides of the petits fours. Store loosely covered with plastic, in the refrigerator for up to 2 days.

NOTES

Both the chocolate ganache and the buttercream need to be smooth and spreadable, so make sure the ganache has cooled to room temperature before using, to prevent it from seeping into the cake.
The chocolate ganache can be made several days in advance and chilled. If you make the ganache beforehand, gently warm it over the lowest heat until it is smooth enough to spread like frosting.
Buttercream can also be made up to 2 weeks in advance and refrigerated, tightly covered, until needed. Let refrigerated buttercream come to room temperature and then briefly rewhip it before using.

Chocolate can be used for many types of desserts. Warm it gently for a smooth and rich topping for ice cream or for chocolate fondue. Let it cool to room temperature and it becomes a glossy, pourable icing. Chill it a bit longer and you can pipe it from a pastry bag to decorate brownies, cupcakes, or cakes.

Noah

Grand Finales

Long before Thanksgiving passes, you can hear Tchaikovsky in the air. His music sets the stage for Nutcracker season, resonating throughout the theatre and the city, and sometimes, when the weather is very brisk, the wind even sounds like the tingling notes from the Sugarplum Fairy's calista. In the cities, everywhere you go seductive smells from street carts, bakeries, and restaurants linger in the air, masking the usual grime and car exhaust with an intoxicating medley of aromas. Festive displays adorn shop windows, trees appear in apartment building entranceways, and chains of little white lights hang along the sidewalks like diamond bracelets. Smoky roasted chestnuts and warm baked bagels, coffee and gourmet cheeses, and spice cakes mingle with the very un-urban scent of newly orphaned pine trees imported from upstate. The trees line the sidewalks like a forest of fresh herbs, and it is the one time of year when it doesn't take the selective perception of a romantic to sense the holiday spirit.

During most of my Nutcracker seasons, Mondays were free and thus reserved for cooking. It was the one day a week I could dabble in the kitchen all day long, interrupted only by the chore of washing leotards or pouring Superglue into pairs of new pointe shoes to harden them. As a student living in New York City, the hardener of choice was a polyurethane floor polish called Fabulon, only the fumes were so strong that the shoes had to be hung out the windows by their ribbons—not the most effective method in a city full of pigeons! To compensate for the smell, I would make pudding or anything fragrant that didn't require much work space and more than a few ingredients to prepare. Unfortunately, living in an apartment without an oven precluded any sort of baking, so that holiday ritual was performed by the French pâtisserie around the corner.

These days, my kitchen is far better equipped, and I can now make at home all those goodies I could once get only at fancy French bakeries or Edgar's on 84th Street. I take particularly guiltless pleasure in stocking my grocery basket with pounds of butter and chocolate, and in making masses of cakes and cookies, remembering the days I used to hike over to the East Side in freezing weather just to buy a certain chocolate torte at my favorite French bakery or indulge in some gargantuan dessert with friends at Serendipity. Dancers have an acute sweet tooth and, during Nut season, a justifiable desire for nibbling more than a mouse's share of little goodies—a high concentration of calories provides energy for short but demanding variations and won't stretch the costume! Perhaps it is the corporeal hyperawareness that results from daily self-dissection in the mirror or simply the fact that anything with sugar just tastes better, but I think most dancers relish desserts in the same way that a diabetic consumes a doughnut—with the greedy pleasure that only forbidden foods can provide. Luckily, spending one's evening waltzing, turning, and jumping in front of an audience prevents most indulgences from ever showing.

Grand Finales celebrates special performances and all your holiday events with equally show-stopping desserts: enjoy classic French choux pastry transformed into stunning cream puffs in Swan Lake. Pear and Hazelnut Marzipan Tart is inspired by one of my first roles in the Nutcracker and is based on a Le Cordon Bleu recipe for a rich butter tart from the Charente region in France. Luxurious Dark Chocolate Pearly Tart is a great make-ahead dessert, while simple and quick Gala Apple Galette is just the thing when you need something quick for surprise guests. But for the times when you really want to pull out all the stops, try my dazzling Chocolate Mousse King, a dense chocolate brownie cake spiraled with rich chocolate mousse and caramel-drizzled raspberries, or five-layer Prince of Almonds Torte with Coffee Buttercream and Chocolate Ganache. And for those truly incorrigible chocoholics, there is none other than the most extravagant mousse cake of all: Chocolate Symphony.

Of all plumed birds, snow white swans have been the consummate symbol of elegance and grace in both classical ballet and cuisine since the Middle Ages. While Louis XIV was developing his court dances in his royal halls in France, the great gourmand king of England, Henry VIII, was enjoying extravagantly choreographed dessert parades of fruits and pastry, often including ornately carved creations of sugar called "deceptions." Emulating the regal posture and stately beauty of swans as models for all sorts of royal confections was the height of culinary chic during this era. Hoffmann even included swans in his idyllic Land of the Sweets.

It was with not so great a leap from the table to the stage that swans were characterized in dance with the great Russian premiere of a full-length Swan Lake in St. Petersburg in 1895. French choreographer Marius Petipa (who had choreographed The Nutcracker three years earlier) and Russian ballet master Lev Ivanov staged a story based on a German fairy tale about a princess named Odette turned into a swan by an evil magician. Swan Lake has become the hallmark of classical ballet, performed more than any other full-length ballet in Russian repertoires, restaged countless times throughout the world with variations in choreography, scenery, and theme.

The idea of embodying avian qualities of movement through jutting wrists and the arch of the neck and shoulders has become a popular vehicle through which to explore the classic themes of romantic love, tragic love, and good versus evil. Choreographic interpretations vary from the seriously traditional (and sometimes painfully long) to the odd, contemporary, and ultra-modern: in 1910, the main role of Prince Siegfried in Diaghilev's Swan Lake was danced by Nijinsky to the Sugarplum Fairy's music from the Nutcracker. Modern-day productions include British choreographer Matthew Bourne's Swan Lake with a completely male cast, while the Australian Dance Theatre's part gymnastic, part breakdance techno-spectacle, Birdbrain, replaces the classic Tchaikovsky music with a bracing score, lightning fast choreography, and no resemblance to the original ballet. Swedish choreographer Mats Ek strips the ballet of both tradition and feathers with his bald and barefoot swans, presenting a prince's psychological journey to maturity. In this version, the conventionally dichotomous black and white swans become dual facets of the same ideal mate, demonstrating the real-world complexities of human emotion and desire. Swan-themed productions have been big ballet business all over the world for centuries. It seems audiences never tire of a good love story, whether between man and woman, man and man, man and swan, or somewhere in between.

This swan-themed dessert will be just as popular a subject for your next gala dinner, made from a quick and easy-to-make pastry called choux, named after the French word for cabbage because of the way it puffs as it bakes. They make a stunning display for any holiday event and will be the talk of bridal showers, birthdays, or Valentine's Day. Serve on a large platter as petits fours, or piped and baked the size of a cream puff (adjust baking times). I've even used them in miniature to surround large sheet cakes. The simple-to-make choux pastry is piped into teardrop shapes and baked, then filled with peppermint whipped cream, made from grinding candy canes into a fine powder.

CHOUX SWANS

pâte à choux (recipe on opposite page)

½ ounce dark chocolate, melted

CANDY CANE CREAM

4 ounces candy canes

2 cups heavy cream, chilled

powdered sugar, for dusting

1. Preheat the oven to 350°F.

2. MAKE THE SWANS: Transfer ¾ of the choux pastry to a pastry bag fitted with a medium-sized star tip.

3. On a well-greased baking sheet, pipe 2-inch-wide by 2½-inch-long teardrop shapes, spacing them 2 inches apart. Bake until golden, 20 to 25 minutes, then flip over with a metal spatula and bake 3 to 5 minutes more, until good and crisp, with a rich, golden brown color on the outside. The shells should sound hollow when tapped with your fingernail. (If you underbake them, they will go soggy faster once filled with the whipped cream.) Cool on racks.

4. Place the remaining choux pastry into another pastry bag containing a small plain tip. Pipe the number 2 elegantly so the top tip forms a small bulb (for the swan's head), arching the body into a gracefully craned neck. Each number 2 should measure about 2 inches from top to bottom. Repeat with the remaining batter, making extras to replace any that may overbake or break. Space them 1 inch apart. Bake for 4 to 5 minutes, until lightly browned. Carefully transfer to racks to cool completely.

5. APPLY CHOCOLATE EYES: To make up the swan faces, melt the chocolate. I find that for such a small amount, the microwave is the best way to do this. Grate the chocolate or cut it into minute little chunks, then microwave for about 2 minutes at the lowest power setting, or until almost melted. Stir until smooth.

6. Dip a toothpick into the chocolate and dab 2 small dots onto the bulb part of each number 2 (the "face" of each swan). Place on racks until the chocolate has set.

7. PREPARE THE CANDY CANE CREAM: For the minty whipped cream, crush the candy canes to a fine powder. (A very clean coffee or spice grinder is perfect for this job. Alternatively, you can place them in a resealable plastic bag and drag a rolling pin back and forth over it until soft and powdery.)

8. Whip the cream to soft peaks with a wire whisk or electric mixer. Sprinkle 2 tablespoons of the candy cane powder over the cream and beat until stiff. Transfer the cream to a pastry bag fitted with a large star tip.

9. ASSEMBLE THE SWANS: To put the swans together (and you'll want to do this shortly before serving so they don't become soggy), cut the teardrop shapes in half widthwise with a sharp serrated knife. Set the bottom half aside and cut the top in half lengthwise, to form two "wings."

10. Pipe the candy cane cream into the base and insert the number 2 piece in the center of the rounded side (see the photo). Top with the 2 wings of each swan. Repeat with the remaining swans. Dust powdered sugar over the tops just before serving.

VARIATION: Vary the flavorings added to the whipped cream to suit different occasions: For bridal showers, Mother's Day, or springtime luncheons, try replacing the powdered candy canes with powdered crystallized violets or rose petals. They add a great Provençal touch, and enhance the cream with a pretty pastel tint and delicate floral flavor. (You can also add a drop or two of food coloring to brighten the color.) Since the little packages often contain mostly broken bits, pulverizing them is also a good way to prevent waste. Grind them to a fine powder and add to the whipped cream to your taste.

Pâte à Choux

This is the dough of éclairs, profiteroles, cream puffs, croquembouche, and savory appetizers like gougères (little puffs of dough usually filled with cheese). It is made quickly on the stove, and since there is no chilling, rolling, or fitting into tins or molds, choux pastry is also one of the easiest doughs to make and probably one of the most versatile.

1 cup water

½ cup (1 stick) unsalted butter, cut into small pieces

½ teaspoon salt

1½ teaspoons sugar

1 cup flour

5 eggs, beaten

1. Combine the water, butter, salt, and sugar in a medium saucepot. Place over medium-high heat and stir until the butter melts.

2. Bring to a boil, then add the flour all at once. Whisk until combined, then reduce the heat to medium-low and cook, stirring, until the dough begins to pull away from the sides of the pot. Switch from the whisk to a wooden spoon and keep paddling the dough from side to side with the spoon for another 2 minutes to cook out the floury taste.

3. Remove from the heat and let cool slightly, then gradually add the beaten eggs, a little at a time, working the batter with the wooden spoon until the eggs are fully incorporated. You want a smooth, thick paste that will pipe easily. Test by scooping up a generous spoonful of the dough and tipping it over. The dough should grudgingly drop off the spoon.

4. At this point you can pipe the dough into shapes and bake according to the recipe you are using or just drop it by spoonfuls onto a greased baking sheet.

5. Set the oven to 350° and bake until the pastry is crisp and golden brown. Makes enough pastry for 1 recipe of Swan Lake.

Pear and Hazelnut Marzipan Tart

1 recipe pâte sucrée (see page 116)

MARZIPAN FILLING

½ cup (1 stick) unsalted butter,
at room temperature

½ cup sugar

2 eggs

½ cup finely ground almonds

¼ cup plus 1 tablespoon finely ground hazelnuts

1 heaping tablespoon flour

half of a perfectly ripe pear

1. Chill the pâte sucrée, roll it out, and fit it into a tart tin as instructed in steps 2 and 3 of the recipe. Do not prebake the tart shell.

2. PREPARE THE MARZIPAN FILLING: In a medium bowl, cream the butter and sugar until light and fluffy, then beat in the eggs. Stir the nuts and flour together, then mix into the batter. (If the nuts aren't already ground, pulse them together in a food processor with a spoonful or two of sugar from the ½ cup you have already measured—the sugar will help keep them from becoming pasty.) Set aside.

3. Spread in the filling in the tart shells and cover loosely with plastic wrap. Chill for several hours or overnight. Beware: If the filling is not thoroughly chilled it will spill over the sides as it bakes.

4. Preheat the oven to 350°F. Slice the pear very thinly and fan it out decoratively across the surface of the chilled tart. Place the tart on a baking sheet and slip it into the oven for 15 minutes, then lower the heat to 300°.

5. Continue baking for about 30 to 35 minutes more, or until the surface becomes golden and dimpled and the tip of a knife inserted into the center comes out clean. Cool for at least 15 minutes before slicing.

In *The Story of the Hard Nut*, Christian Elias Drosselmeyer traveled around the world for a nut hard enough to break the curse on Princess Pirlipat. He roamed for 15 years, searching in London, Paris, and even the Historical Society at Squirreltown. But not all were sympathetic with his plight, and in the unlucky Kingdom of Dates, he was expelled by the Prince of Almonds, who inspired this very welcoming and nutty nibble.

Pâte sucrée

When baked, the texture of this classic sweet dough is like that of a softish shortbread, and if you add a few more tablespoons of sugar, it can be chilled, sliced or rolled out, and baked as cookies. It's buttery flavor makes it perfect for rich nut tarts like the Pear and Hazelnut Marzipan Tart, but if you're looking for a crust without nuts you can substitute it for the nut crust in the Raspberry Linzertorte. This dough should be rolled a bit thicker than you would roll a pie dough, usually about ¼ inch, and is easy to work with as long as it is properly chilled.

½ cup (1 stick) unsalted butter, at room temperature

3 tablespoons sugar

1 egg

¼ teaspoon vanilla extract

7 ounces all purpose flour (about 1⅔ cups sifted)

pinch of salt

1. In a medium bowl, cream the butter and sugar together until light and fluffy. Beat in the egg and vanilla, then add half the flour and the salt. Add the remaining flour and mix just until incorporated. Tread lightly, though; if you overwork the dough, it will get tough. Gather the dough into a ball, then flatten it into a disk and wrap in plastic. Let rest in the refrigerator for at least 30 minutes.

2. Roll out the chilled dough ¼-inch thick, then lay it into your tart tin. I use a 13 ½ by 4-inch rectangular tart pan, but an 8-inch round tin or individual springform tart tins work as well.

3. Once the dough is nicely fitted into the tin, roll a pin across the top to trim off the excess dough, then pierce the base all over with a fork so it doesn't bubble up as it bakes. Chill until ready to fill, then bake as specified in your recipe.

4. If your recipe dictates that the pastry shell should be pre-baked, continue by preheating the oven to 400°F.

5. Fit a sheet of parchment or waxed paper into the base of the well-chilled tart dough. Fill with pastry weights, dried beans, or raw rice. Bake for 10 minutes. Remove the weights and paper and bake for 5 minutes more, until the edges of the dough turn light brown. Remove from the oven and let cool completely on a rack.
Store in an airtight container, or freeze, tightly wrapped, until ready to add your filling.

Makes enough for 1 13 by 4-inch tart shell, with generous trimmings.

Gala Apple Galette

My kind of aromatherapy comes not from scented soaps or smoky incense but from the fragrant trails of cinnamon and nutmeg that fill my kitchen when I bake this heavenly apple galette. The homemade applesauce cooks up quickly but can be replaced with prepared apple butter if you like. It goes almost without saying you'll want to serve it warm out of the oven with vanilla ice cream.

8 ounces frozen puff pastry, thawed to room temperature

APPLESAUCE

3 large Gala apples, peeled, cored and diced

⅓ cup water

½ cup sugar

1 teaspoon lemon juice

½ teaspoon cinnamon

2 large Gala or Granny Smith apples

2 tablespoons sugar

1 tablespoons unsalted butter, cut into small pieces

1. Preheat the oven to 400°F once your puff pastry has thawed completely and can be unrolled without tearing.

2. Place the pastry sheet onto a nonstick baking sheet. Trim the edges to form a circle (or use a 9½-inch plate as a template). Gather and pinch around the circle to form a rim, then slip the baking sheet into the refrigerator for 20 minutes.

3. PREPARE THE APPLESAUCE: Combine the apples, water, sugar, lemon juice, and cinnamon in a medium saucepan. Bring to a boil, then lower the heat and simmer 15 minutes, until the apples are soft. Transfer to a food processor or blender and process to a purée. The consistency should be thick enough spread onto the pastry, not runny. If it is too thin, put the purée back in the pot and cook over low heat for a few more minutes until thickened. Let cool completely.

4. ASSEMBLE THE TART: Core and halve the apples. Slice them as thinly as possible, about ⅛-inch thick. Remove the pastry from the refrigerator. Spread ⅓ cup of the applesauce over the base of the pastry. Fan the apples onto the pastry in a decorative circle, then sprinkle the 2 tablespoons of sugar over the apples and dot with the butter.

4. Bake 25 to 35 minutes, or until puffed and golden brown. Serve warm.

Raspberry Linzertorte

The dough for this stunning raspberry and hazelnut linzertorte is similar to a cookie dough, made by creaming the butter until it is light and fluffy, then adding the remaining ingredients just until incorporated. The result is a rich, beautifully crisp and flavorful base for the thick and tart jam. Because of the high butter content, the dough quickly gets soft, so try to work quickly when handling it. Also, be sure to properly chill the dough or it will be difficult to roll it out—it's best to make it several hours or a day in advance. Luckily, though, the dough is as forgiving as it is delicious, and if you find it tearing as you try to lay it into the tin, simply push the pieces in and press them back together.

HAZELNUT TART SHELL
½ cup (1 stick) unsalted butter, at room temperature

1 egg

½ teaspoon vanilla extract

2 tablespoons heavy cream

½ cup sugar

1 cup toasted and skinned hazelnuts

½ teaspoon ground cinnamon

1 tablespoon unsweetened cocoa powder

2 cups sifted all-purpose flour

FILLING
1¼ cups fine seedless raspberry jam

1 egg yolk

1 teaspoon milk

powdered sugar, for dusting

1. MAKE THE TART SHELL: In a large bowl, cream the butter until light. Add the egg, vanilla, and cream. Mix well.

2. Combine the sugar, hazelnuts, cinnamon, and cocoa powder in the bowl of a food processor and pulse until the nuts are finely ground, then stir into the butter mixture at the lowest speed of your mixer. Mix in the flour just until incorporated. The dough will be sticky, so use a spatula to scoop it onto a piece of heavily floured waxed paper, then lightly knead it into a flat disk and wrap tightly. Chill for at least 1 hour, or overnight before rolling out .

3. When the dough is thoroughly chilled, unwrap it and

place on a generously floured board. Cut off one third of the dough and put it back in the fridge while you roll out the rest. Smooth some flour onto your pin and quickly roll the dough out to ¼ inch thick, turning and flipping it over as you roll so it doesn't stick to your work surface.

4. Place your tart tin over the dough and cut a circle 1 inch larger in diameter than the size of the tin. Fit the circle into the tin (use a spatula to help lift and move the dough), pushing it into the corners so there are no air pockets. If you take some of the trimmings and roll them into a ball, you can use the ball to press the dough into the corners without fear of tearing the dough. When the dough is snug in the tin, roll the pin across the top of the tin to neatly trim the edge. Prick the base all over with a fork. Set aside.

5. Remove the remaining dough from the refrigerator and roll it out slightly thinner than for the base of the tart, about $^3/_8$ inch thick. With a ruler and a sharp knife, cut strips about ¾ inch wide.

6. ADD THE FILLING: Spread the raspberry jam into the base of the tart shell. Lay the strips across the top, crisscrossing them so they form a lattice pattern. Gently pinch the edges to seal the strips to the base. Don't be concerned if the strips don't look absolutely perfect–powdered sugar hides a multitude of sins. Now, this is next step is very important: place the prepared tart in the freezer for 20 minutes.

7. GLAZE AND BAKE THE TART: Just before you are ready to bake the tart, place a baking tray in the oven and preheat to 400°F. In a small bowl, whisk together the egg yolk and 1 teaspoon of milk. Brush over the strips and edge of the tart, covering all visible dough.

8. Place the tart on the baking tray and bake for 15 minutes, then reduce the oven temperature to 375° and continue to bake for 15 to 20 minutes more, or until the crust is golden and the jam is bubbling. Cool thoroughly on a rack, then dust with powdered sugar before slicing.

*T*he pastry chefs watch proudly as the Bon Bons
tumble out from Mother Ginger's skirtfolds.

Mother Ginger Trifle with Chunky Apple Compote and Cognac Custard

Serves 6 to 8

GINGER CAKE

1⅔ cups all-purpose flour

1 teaspoon baking powder

¼ teaspoon baking soda

1½ teaspoons ground ginger

1 teaspoon ground cinnamon

¼ teaspoon ground nutmeg

¼ teaspoon salt

6 tablespoons unsalted butter, at room temperature

½ cup dark brown sugar

2 eggs

½ cup blackstrap molasses

½ cup warm water

COGNAC CUSTARD

8 egg yolks

1 cup sugar

4½ tablespoons all-purpose flour, sifted

3 cups whole milk

¾ teaspoon vanilla extract

2 tablespoons Cognac

CHUNKY APPLE COMPOTE

2 tablespoons unsalted butter

4 Golden Delicious apples, peeled, cored, and diced

¼ cup packed brown sugar

⅓ cup dark raisins

½ teaspoon ground cinnamon

1 tablespoon cognac

TOPPING

1½ cups heavy cream

¼ cup powdered sugar

2 tablespoons sliced almonds

1. MAKE THE GINGER CAKE: Preheat the oven to 350°F. Generously grease and lightly flour an 8-inch square baking pan.

2. In a medium bowl, stir together the flour, baking powder, soda, spices, and salt.
In a large bowl, cream the butter with the brown sugar until light and fluffy. Beat in the eggs, one at a time, then mix in the molasses and warm water. Stir in the flour mixture just until incorporated. Pour into the prepared baking pan. Bake for 30 to 35 minutes, or until the center is springy and a toothpick inserted into the center comes out clean. Let cool on a rack. The cake can be made up to 2 weeks in advance and kept, tightly wrapped in foil, in the freezer.

3. PREPARE THE COGNAC CUSTARD: Combine the egg yolks and sugar in a medium saucepot. Beat until pale and thick, about 3 minutes. Stir in the flour.

4. Add the milk and place over medium heat. Slowly bring to a boil, stirring constantly, then reduce the heat to low and keep whisking for 1 minute more, until thickened. Remove from the heat and stir in the vanilla and Cognac. Pour into a bowl and press a sheet of plastic wrap over the surface. Chill until ready to use.

5. PREPARE THE COMPOTE: In a medium skillet, melt the butter. Add the apples, brown sugar, raisins, and cinnamon and sauté over medium heat for 5 minutes. Raise the heat to high and sprinkle in the Cognac. Let cook for 1 minute more, until most of the liquid is absorbed. Remove from the heat and let cool.

6. ASSEMBLE THE TRIFLE: Cut half of the ginger cake into 2-inch cubes (reserve the rest for another use). Spread half the cubes in the bottom of a 2-quart serving bowl, preferably glass so the creamy layers will be visible (alternatively, divide the cubes among wine glasses for single servings). Spoon half of the compote over the cake, then top with half of the cognac custard. Repeat again, using the rest of the cake, compote, and custard.

7. Cover with plastic wrap and chill in the refrigerator for several hours, so the juices and custard soften the cake.
When you are ready to serve dessert, whip the cream to soft peaks. Add the powdered sugar and keep whipping until stiff. Spoon or pipe the whipped cream over the surface of the trifle and sprinkle the sliced almonds over the top.

Dark Chocolate Pearly Tart

Pearls of white chocolate bejewel this stunning chocolate tart, inspired by Princess Pirlipat. You can use all dark chocolate for the base of this tart or half dark and half bittersweet.

CHOCOLATE FILLING

10 ounces dark or bittersweet chocolate, chopped

1½ cups heavy cream

3 large egg yolks

½ teaspoon vanilla extract

½ recipe Pâte Sucrée, prebaked (page 116), fitted into a 9-inch tart tin and pre-baked

½ ounce white chocolate, melted

whipped cream, for serving

1. MAKE THE FILLING: Place the chocolate and cream in a medium saucepan over very low heat. Stir gently with a whisk until the chocolate is almost melted, then remove from the heat and stir until smooth. Let cool to room temperature, then whisk in the egg yolks and vanilla.

2. ASSEMBLE THE TART: Preheat the oven to 275°F. Place the cooled prebaked tart shell on a baking tray and fill with the chocolate filling. Drip the melted white chocolate in drops of various sizes over the surface.

3. Bake for about 25 minutes, or just until set. Cool completely before slicing. Serve dolloped generously with whipped cream.

Mocha Chestnut Bûche de Noël

MOCHA SPONGE CAKE

¾ cup sifted cake flour

⅓ cup unsweetened cocoa powder

1 cup sugar

2 teaspoons baking powder

½ teaspoon salt

½ teaspoon instant coffee

3 whole eggs

1 tablespoon vanilla extract

½ cup plus 1 tablespoon vegetable oil

5 egg whites

CHOCOLATE CHESTNUT BUTTERCREAM

½ cup canned chestnut purée

¼ cup milk

4 egg whites

¾ cup sugar

1 cup (2 sticks) unsalted butter, at room temperature

8 ounces milk chocolate, melted

MERINGUE MUSHROOMS

3 egg whites, at room temperature

¼ teaspoon cream of tartar

½ cup granulated sugar

⅓ cup powdered sugar

unsweetened cocoa powder, for dusting

GARNISH

fresh rosemary sprigs dusted with powdered sugar

NOTE: For the cake, use a 12 by 17-inch jelly roll pan. To make the meringue mushrooms, you will need a pastry bag with no. 6 tip, 2 large baking sheets, and parchment paper.

1. MAKE THE SPONGE CAKE: Preheat the oven to 350°F. Line a greased 12 by 17-inch jelly roll pan with a sheet of waxed paper, then butter the waxed paper.

2. In a medium bowl, stir together the sifted cake flour, cocoa powder, ¾ cup sugar (reserve ¼ cup sugar to beat into the egg whites), baking powder and salt. Set aside.

3. In a large bowl, sprinkle the instant coffee over the whole eggs, vanilla extract and vegetable oil. Let the coffee dissolve, then mix with an electric mixer on medium-high speed for 2 minutes. Stir in the flour mixture just until incorporated.

4. In a separate clean and very dry bowl, beat the egg whites on medium speed until frothy. Turn the mixer speed to high and gradually add the remaining ¼ cup sugar, beating until the egg whites form stiff peaks.

5. Stir a large dollop of the egg whites into the batter and mix well, then gently fold in the remaining whites. Pour the batter into the prepared pan and bake for 15 to 18 minutes, until the cake springs back when light pushed with your fingertip.

6. Remove the cake from the oven and let rest until cool enough to handle. Invert the cake onto a dish towel. Remove the waxed paper, then roll the cake up in the towel into a cylinder. Place seam side down and let rest until cool.

7. MAKE THE CHESTNUT BUTTERCREAM: In a small saucepan, whisk the chestnut purée and milk together over medium-low heat until you have a smooth paste. Set aside to cool.

8. Place the egg whites and sugar in a large bowl set over simmering water, and whisk occasionally until the sugar has dissolved.
Remove from the heat and beat over high speed until stiff, glossy peaks form.

9. Beat in the softened butter, a tablespoon at a time, until smooth, then add the cooled chestnut paste. (Don't worry if the mixture looks like it is separating; just keep beating until it becomes smooth again.) Beat in the melted milk chocolate. Chill until ready to use.

10. PREPARE THE MERINGUE MUSHROOMS: Preheat the oven to 225°F. Beat the egg whites in a very clean, dry bowl until frothy. Add the cream of tartar and keep beating, gradually incorporating the granulated sugar until the egg whites are stiff and glossy. Fold in the powdered sugar.

11. Transfer the egg whites to a pastry bag fitted with a plain no. 6 (8mm) tip.
Line 2 large baking sheets with parchment paper. On the first sheet, pipe 48 mushroom caps, ranging from 1 to 1½ inches wide and about ¾ inch high, spacing them about ½ inch apart.

12. Smooth over the top of each cap with a finger dipped in cold water to get rid of any peaks. Lightly flick a little cocoa powder through a sifter over the caps and set aside.

13. On the second sheet, pipe the stems. You will need 48 of these also, spaced ½ inch apart, each about ½ inch wide at one end and tapering off to a point, ¾ inch long in total. The sizes can vary along with the sizes of the mushroom caps, so that some are slightly larger than others. Set the remaining meringue aside.

14. Place the mushroom caps on the center rack of the oven, with the stems on the rack beneath it. Bake for 25 to 30 minutes, until the stems are dried and stiff. Remove the stems from the oven and continue to bake the caps for another 20 to 25 minutes, until firm.

15. Remove the caps from the oven and loosen them with a spatula. With the tip of a sharp knife, twist a small hole into the flat part of each cap. Dab a little of the remaining meringue onto the tip of a stem and insert the stem into the hole. Repeat with the remaining mushroom caps, so you have 48 stemmed mushrooms in all (more than enough for one bûche de noël, so don't worry if a few of them break).

16. Return the stemmed mushrooms to the oven for 15 more minutes, until the meringue "glue" has dried completely. Remove from the oven and let cool.

17. TO ASSEMBLE THE BÛCHE DE NOËL: Unroll the cooled cake and remove the dish towel. Spread the inside of the cake with half of the chestnut buttercream, then reroll into a cylinder. Chill for about 30 minutes.

18. When the buttercream is firm, transfer the log to a serving plate or cutting board. Diagonally slice off one end and replace it along the side of the log to form a "branch." Ice the top and sides with the remaining buttercream, using a knife or spatula to make rough strokes to look like the bark of a tree. Chill for at least 1 hour or up to overnight before slicing.

19. Garnish the cake with the meringue mushrooms and sugared rosemary sprigs. Serve with extra meringue mushrooms alongside.

Chocolate Mousse King

The Mouse King squeezed himself through a hole into Marie's room, looking to satiate his ravenous appetite for sweets: "Out with your cakes, marzipan and sugarstick, gingerbread cakes! Don't pause to argue! If yield them you won't, I'll chew up Nutcracker! See if I don't!"

In 19th-century Europe mice were a common household nuisance, so a mouse king was a logical fairytale nemesis for the Nutcracker. This royally decadent chocolate extravaganza looks spectacular but still has the comforting appeal of a homemade cake. A dense, fudgy brownie base enveloped in a satiny bittersweet glaze and crowned with spires of thick chocolate mousse surrounds a dome of fresh raspberries drizzled with caramel syrup. This is the perfect treat for chocoholics during the holidays, on Valentine's Day, or any time you're in need of a serious chocolate fix. Serve in a puddle of fresh raspberry coulis to balance the richness of the chocolate.

BROWNIE CAKE

½ cup (1 stick) unsalted butter

2 ounces bittersweet chocolate

2 eggs

½ cup granulated sugar

1/3 cup dark brown sugar

2 teaspoons vanilla extract

6 tablespoons all purpose flour

1 teaspoon baking powder

¼ cup unsweetened cocoa powder

pinch of salt

BITTERSWEET CHOCOLATE MOUSSE

6 ounces bittersweet chocolate

3 egg yolks

½ cup heavy cream

½ teaspoon vanilla extract

½ teaspoon instant coffee

3 egg whites

½ cup sugar

CHOCOLATE GLAZE

1 cup heavy cream

2 tablespoons unsalted butter

2 tablespoons sugar

10 ounces dark or bittersweet chocolate, chopped

GARNISH

1 pint fresh raspberries

1/3 cup sugar

2 tablespoons water

silver dragées, for decoration (optional)

RASPBERRY COULIS

2 pints raspberries or 1 pound bag frozen, thawed

½ cup sugar

1 teaspoon fresh lemon juice

1. MAKE THE BROWNIE CAKE: Preheat the oven to 325°F. Generously grease an 8-inch springform pan and line it with parchment paper, then grease the paper.

2. Melt the butter and bittersweet chocolate together in a small saucepan over low heat. Set aside.

3. In a medium bowl, beat the eggs together with both sugars and the vanilla vigorously for 2 minutes. Stir in the melted butter and chocolate.

4. Sift together the flour, baking powder, cocoa, and salt and fold into the chocolate batter, then pour into the prepared springform pan.

5. Bake for 20 to 25 minutes, or just until a toothpick inserted into the center comes out clean. The consistency should be dense and fudgy like a chewy brownie, but not undercooked or the batter will ooze out of the center when it is sliced. Invert onto a rack and remove the springform pan. Let cool thoroughly before removing the parchment paper.

6. MAKE THE CHOCOLATE MOUSSE: Melt the chocolate gently in a double boiler. Let cool, then beat in the 3 egg yolks, one at a time, until the mixture is smooth.

7. In a small saucepan, combine 1 tablespoon of the heavy cream with the vanilla extract and instant coffee. Stir over low heat until the coffee is dissolved. Stir this mixture into the melted chocolate. Set aside while you beat the egg whites and cream.

8. In another spotlessly clean, dry bowl (if it is moist or the least bit greasy, the whites won't inflate), whip the egg whites until foamy. Sprinkle in the sugar, a little at a time, and keep beating until stiff. Scoop out a large dollop and work it into the chocolate mixture to loosen it up, then fold in the remaining egg whites, this time gently, to keep the batter light.

9. In one last bowl, beat the remaining chilled heavy cream until stiff enough to hold its shape, then fold it also into the chocolate. Cover and chill for at least 1 hour or up to 1 day.

10. MAKE THE CHOCOLATE GLAZE: Combine the cream, butter, and sugar in a saucepan. Stir over medium heat until the sugar is dissolved. Bring to just under a boil, then remove the pot from the heat. Add the chopped chocolate. Stir gently with a whisk until smooth. Let cool to room temperature.

11. DRAPE THE CAKE WITH THE CHOCOLATE GLAZE: Peel the parchment off the cooled cake, then turn it back over on the rack. Place the rack on a baking tray. Pour the chocolate glaze over the cake, starting from the center and tipping the rack slightly back and forth so the glaze spills over the edges and coats the cake completely.

12. Refrigerate until the glaze has set, then repeat once again for a smooth, satiny finish (you can reuse the extra glaze that has spilled onto the baking sheet). Chill until set.

13 ASSEMBLE AND DECORATE THE CAKE: Fit a piping bag with an extra-large decorative tip of your choice and fill the bag with the chocolate mousse. Pipe large swirls around the edge of the cake, then fill it in the center with the remaining mousse.

14. Use a spatula to make a well in the center of the mousse, then fill with the fresh raspberries, mounding them into the dome of a crown. If you don't have a piping bag, you can make an equally stunning, albeit rustic creation by just scooping large dollops of the mousse onto the surface of the cake and running around the edge with a spatula, then piling the raspberries into the center. The berries will fill in any rough edges, and, of course, the finished product will taste just as good.

15. MAKE THE CARAMEL CRACKLE GARNISH: In a small saucepan, bring the sugar and water to a boil over high heat. The pot can be shaken a little, but don't stir or the sugar will crystallize. Cook until you have a light golden syrup, about 5 minutes. Cool slightly, then drizzle over the berries and let harden to a thin, crackly coating.

16. If you like, you can top the spirals of mousse with silver dragées. Chill until ready to serve.

17. MAKE THE RASPBERRY COULIS: Place the raspberries, sugar, and lemon juice in a blender and process on high speed until smooth. Pass the mixture through a fine-mesh sieve to remove the seeds. Store in the refrigerator, tightly covered, for up to 1 week. Spoon some of the coulis onto individual plates and top with slices of the cake

Prince of Almonds Torte with Coffee Buttercream and Chocolate Ganache

ALMOND CAKE

8 egg yolks

1¼ cups sugar

⅔ cup finely crushed day-old Italian breadcrumbs

2 teaspoons almond extract

¼ cup cake flour

2 teaspoons baking powder

¼ cup milk

2 cups blanched almonds, finely ground

14 egg whites

½ teaspoon salt

¼ teaspoon cream of tartar

CHOCOLATE GANACHE ICING

20 ounces bittersweet chocolate

2 cups heavy cream

¼ cup (½ stick) unsalted butter

¼ cup sugar

COFFEE BUTTERCREAM FILLING

4 egg yolks

2 eggs

1 cup sugar

2 teaspoons instant coffee

1 tablespoon warm milk

2 cups (4 sticks) unsalted butter, at room temperature

chocolate shavings, for the side of the cake, optional

caramel shards for garnish (see page134)

1. PREPARE THE ALMOND CAKE: Preheat the oven to 350°F. Butter two 9-inch nonstick cake pans, then line the bottoms with buttered parchment paper. You will be reusing the pans, along with the rounds of paper, until you have made 5 layers.

2. In a large bowl, beat the egg yolks with 1 cup of the sugar until pale and thick. Stir in the breadcrumbs and almond extract and beat until smooth.
Sift the cake flour with the baking powder, then add to the batter alternately with the milk. Stir in the ground almonds.

3. In another large bowl, whip the egg whites with the salt and cream of tartar until soft peaks form, then sprinkle in the remaining ¼ cup sugar and beat until stiff.

4. Stir a few spoonfuls of whipped egg whites into the almond batter to loosen it up, then fold in the remaining egg whites just until incorporated. If you overmix, the cake will not rise, so blend gently but thoroughly. Divide two fifths of the batter evenly between the cake pans.

5. Bake for 10 to 12 minutes, or until the center is golden and springy. Run a knife around the edge of each pan, then turn the cakes out onto racks to cool. Gently remove the parchment paper (this is easier to do when the cake is still warm), then cool completely before icing. Repeat with the remaining batter for 3 more layers.

6. PREPARE THE CHOCOLATE GANACHE: Break the chocolate into small pieces. Combine the cream, butter, and sugar in a medium saucepan and place over medium heat. Stir just until the butter is melted and the sugar has dissolved.

Remove the pot from the heat and add the chocolate. Cover the pan and let stand for 5 minutes, then stir gently with a whisk or wooden spoon until the chocolate is melted and the icing is smooth. If using right away, chill it a bit until thickened enough to pour without soaking into the cake–it should be the consistency of loosely flowing honey.

7. PREPARE THE COFFEE BUTTERCREAM: Place the yolks, whole eggs, and sugar in a double boiler over simmering water and stir to dissolve the sugar until the mixture reaches 110°F. Remove from the heat and beat until light and thick.

8. In a small bowl, stir the coffee into the milk to dissolve it, then blend into the beaten eggs.

9. In a large bowl, cream the butter until light. Gradually beat in the egg mixture until thick and smooth.
Coffee buttercream can be made up to 1 week ahead. Keep refrigerated, tightly covered with plastic wrap, until needed.

10. If you have made the ganache and buttercream ahead of time, bring them to room temperature and beat until smooth before using.

11. ASSEMBLE THE CAKE: Place pieces of parchment or waxed paper along the edges of a serving dish and top with the first cake layer. This will keep the dish clean while you ice and decorate the cake.

12. Spread about ½ cup of the coffee buttercream evenly over the first layer, and top with the second layer. Repeat with 2 more layers, then top with the last cake layer. Smooth any buttercream that is left around the sides of the cake to fill in any gaps. Chill in the refrigerator for 1 hour.

13. Pour enough ganache over the center of the cake to run off the sides, then spread with a knife or offset spatula to coat the sides completely.

14. Chill the cake for 15 minutes, then either press chocolate shavings or spread more ganache onto the sides of the cake. For an even grander pièce de résistance, pipe additional ganache decoratively with a pastry bag fitted with star-shaped tip, and top with shards of caramel sugar.

Caramel Decorations

Crowning a cake with a sparkling tiara of caramelized sugar is a great way to add a glamorous garnish to a cake–and doesn't require any special talent to make.

To prepare the caramel, have ready a large baking tray that has been heavily rubbed with vegetable oil.
For the caramel, bring ½ cup sugar and ¼ cup water to a boil in a small, heavy saucepan. Stir until the sugar is dissolved, then let boil untouched until the sugar turns light brown. Swirl the pan gently if you find the sugar darkening unevenly.
Remove the caramel from the heat and pour it onto the baking tray. The effect you achieve will depend on how you pour. You can drizzle the sugar very thinly for a delicate and lacy webbed effect or be more heavy-handed for thicker shards, or pour the caramel in short drops to harden into amber "jewels." Once the caramel has hardened completely, gently lift one edge with a spatula and break it into pieces to arrange on the top or sides of your cake.

Store the caramel between sheets of waxed paper in an air-tight container for up to 1 day. To prevent the caramel from becoming moist and sticky, store it at room temperature and garnish the cake just before serving.

Orange Entrechat Quatre Cake

This buttery cake gets its name from the French quatre-quarts gâteau, or "four quarters" cake, an old-fashioned pound cake containing a base of four ingredients in equal amounts: flour, sugar, butter, and eggs. A silky orange icing embellishes the cake in a sugary ripple, just enough accessory to justify it as a party dessert. But don't stop there: add berries and cream for a summer strawberry shortcake, or skip the icing and use it instead of sponge cake in trifle. Slice thickly as a base for baked Alaska, or cut it into cubes and dip them into chocolate fondue. The balletic title reflects the four principal ingredients in the cake, representing the four beats of the legs in the jump by the same name.

ORANGE CAKE

1 cup plus 1 tablespoon sugar

2 cups all-purpose flour, sifted

1 tablespoon baking powder

¼ teaspoon salt

1 cup (2 sticks) unsalted butter, at room temperature

4 large eggs

½ cup orange juice

⅓ cup sour cream

1 tablespoon vanilla extract

finely grated zest of 1 orange

ORANGE GLAZE

2 cups powdered sugar

¼ cup fresh orange juice, strained through a fine sieve

1. MAKE THE CAKE: Preheat the oven to 350°F. Generously butter a 9-inch Bundt pan. Toss in 1 tablespoon of sugar and shake the pan around to coat it evenly. Set aside.

2. Sift the flour, baking powder, and salt together. Set aside.

3. Beat the butter and remaining 1 cup sugar in a large mixing bowl until light. Gradually add the eggs, one at a time, and beat until the batter is fluffy.
In a medium bowl, combine the orange juice, sour cream, vanilla, and orange zest and mix into the batter alternately with the sifted flour. Pour into the prepared pan

4. Bake for 40 to 45 minutes, or until a cake tester inserted into the middle of the cake comes out clean. Run a knife around the sides of the pan and invert the cake onto a rack to cool.

5. GLAZE THE CAKE: Whisk the powdered sugar and orange juice together in a small bowl until smooth. Place the cake on a rack over a baking sheet. Prick the top of the cake all over with a toothpick. Drizzle the glaze over the cake, so it dribbles down the sides and into the toothpick holes. Let stand for at least 15 minutes to let the glaze set.

Black Forest Crêpe Gâteau

This dazzling finale updates the classic German layered whipped cream, cherry, and chocolate Schwarzenwald-kuchen, or Black Forest cake, replacing the dense kirsch-soaked layers of chocolate cake with thin chocolate crêpes. It is a relatively simple cake to put together using a 9½-inch crêpe pan and a 9-inch springform pan, and the result is fabulously impressive. A mild cherry liqueur called Danish Kirsberry adds just the right amount of cherry essence without tasting too strongly of alcohol. Kirsberry is mellower than the German cherry brandy called kirschwasser, but if you can't find it, any cherry liqueur, Chambord, or crème de cassis will make a fine substitute. This cake tastes best the same day it is made.

CRÊPES

12 eggs

1¾ cups all-purpose flour

6 tablespoons unsweetened cocoa powder

¾ cup sugar

¾ teaspoon salt

2½ cups plus 2 tablespoons milk

1¼ cups heavy cream

5 tablespoons unsalted butter, melted

3 tablespoons Kirsberry cherry liqueur, or Chambord

2 teaspoons unsalted butter

WHIPPED CREAM FILLING

2½ cups heavy cream

¾ cup powdered sugar

3 tablespoons Kirsberry cherry liqueur, Kirsch, or Chambord

16 ounce jar Moreno cherries

3 ounce bar or block of bittersweet chocolate, for shavings

GLAZE

½ cup cherry or currant jelly

3 tablespoons water

powdered sugar, for dusting

1. MAKE THE CRÊPES: Place the eggs, flour, cocoa, sugar, and salt in a medium bowl. Beat at medium speed until you have a smooth batter. Slowly beat in the milk and heavy cream. Stir in the melted butter, then the liqueur. Let rest for 1 hour at room temperature, loosely covered with plastic.

2. Place a crêpe pan over medium heat. (You could save a lot of time here by doing double duty with 2 crêpe pans.) Add the remaining 2 teaspoons butter and swirl to coat the bottom, then pour off any excess so the pan is just lightly greased. Now add about ⅓ cup of the batter to the pan and quickly tip the pan from side to side to coat the bottom evenly.

3. When the edges begin to turn brown (this should take about 1 minute), slide a spatula underneath the center of the crêpe and flip it over. If you lift just the edge, it usually tears the crêpe, so slide the spatula as far as you can before turning it over. Cook for another minute, just until lightly browned, then transfer to a sheet of parchment or waxed paper to cool. Don't worry if the first crêpe doesn't work; there is usually one casualty before the pan is properly warmed up to cook.

Watch carefully and adjust the heat if the crêpes brown too quickly—you want the surface lightly veined, not charred. Repeat with the remaining batter.

Crêpes can be made up to a month in advance and frozen, layered between waxed paper and tightly wrapped in foil.

4. WHIP THE CREAM: Prepare the gâteau filling by whipping the cream to soft peaks. Sift in the sugar, then add the liqueur, and continue to whip until stiff. Chill until ready to assemble the cake.

5. ASSEMBLE THE CAKE: Grease a 9-inch springform pan and line with plastic wrap so it hangs far enough over the edges to be folded over the top of the cake. Reserve 4 or 5 good-looking crêpes for decorating the top of the finished cake.

6. Line the pan with 4 crêpes, overlapping so they hang over the edges of the pan, leaving the center of the base bare. The crêpes need to hang over enough so they can be folded back over the top of the finished cake. Place a fifth crêpe over the bottom of the pan to cover the bald spot. Spread this crêpe with about ⅓ cup of whipped cream, enough to generously cover the bottom about ¼ inch thick.

7. Drain the cherries, then slice them into slivers and sprinkle a couple of spoonfuls over the cream.

8. MAKE THE CHOCOLATE SHAVINGS: Now take a vegetable peeler and shave the slab of chocolate, dragging the blade over the edge of the bar until you have a tablespoon or so of chocolate shavings. Scatter the shavings over the cherries and cream. Top with another crêpe and press gently to remove any excess air. Top with the whipped cream, slivered cherries, and shaved chocolate as before. Repeat with the remaining crêpes, layering the cream, cherries, and shaved chocolate, up to the top of the pan.

9. Fold the first 4 crêpes (which have been hanging over the sides) over on the top of the cake. Wrap with the over-hanging plastic and chill for 2 to 3 hours.

10. After the gâteau is fully chilled, remove the springform pan and plastic wrap and place on a serving dish. Make the glaze by heating the cherry or currant jelly with the water in a small pot over low heat, stirring, just until it reaches a boil. Remove from the heat and pour through a fine strainer into a bowl. Arrange the reserved crêpes decoratively over the top of the cake. Brush the top and sides with the cooled glaze.

11. Decorate the top with more chocolate shavings and heavy shakes of powdered sugar.

Chocolate Symphony

This quartet of white and bittersweet chocolates can only be described as music to your mouth. Dense, rich layers of chocolate cake are alternated with white chocolate and bittersweet mousses and buttercream, then luxuriously enrobed with smooth bittersweet glaze. Both the mousses and the buttercreams can be made in advance to make life easier, but prepare the glaze just before you are ready to use it so it will be at the perfect temperature to pour over the assembled and chilled cake.

CHOCOLATE CAKE

1 cup (2 sticks) unsalted butter

8 ounces bittersweet chocolate

4 eggs

4 egg yolks

½ cup sugar

2 heaping tablespoons all-purpose flour

WHITE CHOCOLATE BUTTERCREAM

1 egg

2 egg yolks

½ cup sugar

¾ cup (1½ sticks) unsalted butter, at room temperature

3 ounces white chocolate, melted

BITTERSWEET CHOCOLATE MOUSSE

7 ounces bittersweet chocolate

1 cup plus 2 tablespoons heavy cream

1 tablespoon amaretto liqueur

WHITE CHOCOLATE MOUSSE

4 ounces white chocolate

½ cup heavy cream

BITTERSWEET CHOCOLATE GLAZE

10 ounces bittersweet chocolate, chopped

½ cup plus 2 tablespoons evaporated milk

2 teaspoons vanilla extract

3 tablespoons unsalted butter, cut into 3 pieces

1. MAKE THE CHOCOLATE CAKE: Preheat the oven to 350°F. Butter 2 9-inch cake pans and cover the bases with a round of parchment paper. Add a spoonful of flour and shake the pans around to coat the sides, then tap out the excess.

2. In a small saucepan, melt the butter and chocolate together over low heat while you beat the eggs, egg yolks, and sugar together in a stainless bowl set over, but not touching simmering water. Beat them until they are very thick and light.

3. Gently stir in the melted chocolate, then fold in the flour. You just want to bring the ingredients together, not mix so vigorously that you deflate the loftily whipped eggs. Divide half the batter evenly among the baking pans (baking 2 at a time to make 4 layers).

4. Bake for 15 minutes, or until a toothpick poked into the center of each cake comes out clean. Invert the layers onto a rack to cool. Gently remove the parchment rounds and reuse for the remaining layers.

5. MAKE THE WHITE CHOCOLATE BUTTERCREAM: Combine the egg and the yolks with the sugar in a double boiler set over simmering water. With an electric mixer, beat until thick and light and the batter dribbles in ribbons when the beaters are lifted. Set aside.

6. In a medium bowl, cream the butter until light. Gradually beat in the egg mixture, then the melted white chocolate until light, thick, and smooth. Use immediately or refrigerate, tightly covered with plastic wrap. Bring to room temperature and stir until smooth before spreading onto your cake.

7. MAKE THE BITTERSWEET CHOCOLATE MOUSSE: Melt the chocolate along with 2 tablespoons heavy cream very gently over simmering water. Let cool.

8. In a medium bowl, whip the remaining 1 cup cream with the amaretto to stiff peaks. Gently fold in the melted chocolate. Chill until ready to use.

9. MAKE THE WHITE CHOCOLATE MOUSSE: Melt the white chocolate with 2 tablespoons of the heavy cream over very low heat. Stir until smooth.

10. In a medium bowl, whip the remaining heavy cream to stiff peaks. Gently fold in the melted chocolate. Chill until ready to use.

11. MAKE THE BITTERSWEET CHOCOLATE GLAZE: Combine the chocolate and half of the evaporated milk in a small saucepan. Let the chocolate melt very gently until almost melted, then remove from the heat and whisk in the remaining ingredients until smooth. Cool for a few minutes before using.

12. ASSEMBLE THE CAKE: Once you have all the components of the Symphony prepared, begin by spreading 3 of the 4 cake layers with the white chocolate buttercream, reserving about ½ cup to fill any gaps later on. Chill the layers until the buttercream is firm.

13. Next, spread 2 of the layers with the bittersweet mousse,

and the third with the white mousse. Sandwich the layers together, with the white mousse layer in the middle, then fill in the sides with the reserved buttercream. Chill the cake for several hours before coating with the glaze.

14. Slide the thoroughly chilled unglazed cake onto a rack and place a baking tray underneath. Pour the bittersweet glaze over the top of the cake slowly but steadily, so it coats the top and falls down the sides seamlessly. Gently smooth the sides with an offset spatula if any spots need covering. Place the rack with the cake in the refrigerator until the glaze is set.

15. When the glaze is firm, lift the cake off the rack and slide it onto a cake dish. Scrape the excess glaze off the baking tray and transfer it to a pastry bag fitted with a decorative tip. I use a star tip to make swirls on the top of the cake and a small plain tip for dots along the base. There should be just enough glaze left to decorate the cake.

NOTE: The musical chocolate decorations on the top of the cake were made by spreading transfer sheets with tempered bittersweet chocolate (*see tempering chocolate, page 91*). Transfer sheets are made by a special machine that sprays clear acetate decoratively with cocoa butter; they are available at specialty bakeware shops.

Dessert Sauces

Berry Coulis

Only if you have bushels of your own berries or you can buy them very cheap should you make this versatile puréed dessert sauce from fresh berries. In fact, frozen berries are preferable for such sauces–they tend to yield more juice when thawed, are more economical, and are available year-round. A coulis can be made from any juicy fruit, preferably those with vibrant colors like black-berries, raspberries, or strawberries, although kiwis and ripe mangoes work well, too. The purpose of a coulis is mainly to balance the richness and provide contrast with the color of the dessert it surrounds. The sauce should be made from a fruit that complements the dessert; for example, raspberries with chocolate, or tropical fruits with coconut-based custards or cakes.

Add a few drops of lemon juice to the coulis, if you like, and store it covered or in a plastic squeeze bottle for easy serving.

1 bag (16 ounces) frozen blackberries, raspberries, or strawberries, thawed
¼ cup sugar

Place the berries and sugar in a medium saucepan over low heat. Stir, mashing with a fork, until the sugar is dissolved, then remove from the heat. Purée in a food processor or blender, then press through a fine sieve to remove the seeds. Pour the coulis into a small bowl (discarding the seeds) and cover with plastic wrap. Keep chilled until ready to serve.

Store for up to a week in the refrigerator or up to one month in the freezer.

Thinner Chocolate Ganache

Ganache is basically a mixture of chocolate and cream. Depending on the temperature and the ratio of cream to chocolate, it performs a variety of functions: serving as a sauce, glaze, frosting, or filling. In this recipe, half and half is used to make a smooth, pourable sauce for ice cream and cakes, or the dipping sauce for a dessert fondue.

1 cup half and half
10 ounces rich milk chocolate, chopped into small pieces

Stir the half and half and chocolate together in a medium saucepan over low heat until smooth. Serve warm or at room temperature.
Makes approximately 1¾ cups.

Rich Chocolate Sauce

Substitute heavy cream for the half and half and bittersweet chocolate for the milk chocolate in the recipe above.

White Chocolate Sauce

1 ½ cups half and half
8 ounces white chocolate, broken into little bits

Stir the half and half and chocolate together over low heat until smooth. Serve at room temperature or chilled.
Makes approximately 1 ¾ cups.

Chai Crème Anglaise

Chai spices make a basic dessert sauce a little more special, suited to serving with desserts like the Pear and Hazelnut Marzipan Tart.

1 cup milk
¾ cup heavy cream
2 cinnamon sticks
4 whole cloves
4 large egg yolks
¼ cup sugar

Combine the milk, heavy cream, cinnamon sticks, and cloves in a medium pot and bring to a simmer. Turn the heat to its lowest setting, just so it bubbles lazily, and let the spices infuse the mixture for 15 minutes.

Pour through a fine sieve into a bowl and discard the spices. In another bowl, beat the egg yolks and sugar until thick and light. Add a little of the infused cream and mix well. Gradually add the rest of the cream, stirring constantly so the eggs don't cook. Pour back into the pot and cook over medium heat, stirring, until the sauce thickens enough to coat the back of a wooden spoon. Pass through a sieve again, if you like, and let cool. Store in the refrigerator for up to 3 days.

Makes 2 cups.

Vanilla Caramel Sauce

Here is a basic sauce that you can use for all sorts of desserts. Pour over ice cream, use as a dip for apples or cakes alongside chocolate fondue sauces, or serve drizzled next to your favorite slice of cake.

¾ cup sugar
¼ cup water
3 tablespoons unsalted butter
1 cup heavy cream
½ teaspoon vanilla extract

Combine the sugar and water in a medium saucepan. Place over low heat and stir until the sugar has dissolved, then raise the heat to high and let the sugar bubble away vigorously for 5 minutes. Brush down any splatters on the sides of the pan with a pastry brush dipped in water. Continue to boil until the sugar begins to turn from clear to light golden, and when it reaches a rich amber color, take the pot off the heat. Add the butter and cream and cover. Set aside for 5 minutes, then slowly stir with a wooden spoon until smooth and glossy. Mix in the vanilla. Serve warm.

Store, tightly covered, in the refrigerator for up to 1 week. To reheat, microwave on low power in 30-second intervals, stirring in between until the sauce is smooth and pourable. Makes about 1½ cups.

Pineapple Caramel Sauce

Prepare the Vanilla Caramel Sauce above, substituting ¼ cup pineapple juice and ¾ cup heavy cream for the 1 cup heavy cream.

Glossary

EQUIPMENT AND INGREDIENTS

Baking pans: The only thing more frustrating than not having the right ingredients for a recipe is not having the proper pans to bake it in. Having a basic stock of bakeware will get you through most of the recipes in this book—the more unusual tools and gadgets like gingerbread molds, cannoli tubes, or other such trinkets, albeit wonderful for their purpose, have been avoided in this book for the practical reason that you most likely will not have them in your own kitchen. Non-stick versions of the following pans can be helpful but are not necessary—a little butter for greasing and a sheet of parchment or waxed paper provide adequate security that your baked goods will release easily from their pans. Nonstick or not, it is better to have a few good pans than a wide assortment of inferior ones. This is especially true of flat baking sheets—the cheap ones will burn your cookies faster, bake unevenly, and warp in the oven. Invest in 2 good sheets and you will be eternally grateful. Here is a list of the most basic baking pans you will need:

13 by 9 by 2-inch glass or ceramic baking dish (doubles as a roasting pan, lasagna or casserole dish, and serving dish).
9-inch round cake pans (2 or 3); an extra pair of cake pans saves baking time when making multi-tiered cakes such as the Prince of Almonds Torte or the Chocolate Symphony).
9-inch springform pan
heavy baking sheets (2 or 3), approximately 12 inches long and 18 inches wide, the heavier the better.
9-inch tart tin with removable bottom
Nonstick loaf pan.
Parchment paper or waxed paper for lining pans. Both are reusable and provide a nonstick barrier between cakes and cookies and baking pans. Waxed paper is less expensive, but it can burn at higher temperatures and can leave a greasy residue on pans.

4-ounce ceramic ramekins (8), versatile since they are attractive enough for baking and serving soufflés and puddings, can be used as molds, or for holding ingredients for mise en place, as well as for such savory purposes as serving dipping sauces, olives, nuts, or butter.

optional/additional:
8 or 9-inch crêpe pan
cloth or disposable pastry bag with bakers tips in various shapes and sizes (one small and one large plain tip and a small star-shaped tip).

Bowls: I prefer stainless bowls to glass or plastic, since they are unbreakable, sturdy, and don't stain or retain food odors. Placed over a pot of simmering water, they perform well as a double boiler, and can be immersed right into ice water for quick cooling, all in the same bowl. A very basic set should include a small, medium, and large bowl for mixing batters.

Chocolate: see pages 90-91.

Chocolate shavings: To make chocolate shavings to decoratively scatter over a cake, you'll need a thick chunk or bar of fine-quality room-temperature chocolate. If the chocolate is too cold, the shavings will look brittle and jagged, and if it is too warm, they won't hold their shape. Shave the edge with a vegetable peeler firmly and deliberately, from one side edge to another, onto waxed paper. Keep the shaved chocolate chilled until ready to use. To apply the shavings to cakes or desserts, use a flat or offset spatula to lift them off the waxed paper and press them against the sides of the cake or scatter them over a tart, so the heat from your fingers doesn't melt the chocolate.

Citrus fruit: Out-of-season citrus fruit like lemons and limes may need some coaxing before they release their juice. To maximize their juice yield, roll each fruit under your palm with steady pressure two or three times to loosen the membranes or microwave the fruit whole on high power for 10 to 15 seconds before reaming.

Clarified butter: By removing the solids and water from hard sticks of butter, you can cook at a higher temperature without the danger of burning and lend luxurious buttery flavor to your recipe. Clarified butter is great for cooking crêpes, pancakes, omelettes, and vegetables and for pan-frying fish and is quick and easy to make in the microwave:
Place a stick of room-temperature unsalted butter in a small microwavable glass bowl. Heat on medium power until completely melted. If you use a glass bowl, you will see that the butter cleanly separates into two layers: pure liquid gold on the bottom and frothy white milk solids on the top. Carefully remove from the oven and skim off the froth—the golden liquid underneath is what you want. Store in a jar in the refrigerator or freezer.

Crêpe pan: I use this wide, flat pan with its low, curved edge as much for making pancakes as for frying eggs, making crab cakes and fritters, sautéing bananas or anything done with a frying pan. Buy at least an 8-inch or bigger pan so the crêpes will be large enough to fold and enclose a filling. Nonstick can be useful but is not necessary if you properly proof your pan. (See page 73 for crêpe techniques.)

Double boiler: Whether you buy a specifically designed pot set or fashion your own from a pot and a snug-fitting stainless steel bowl, a double boiler is indispensable for heating delicate mixtures like crème anglaise or melting chocolate. Cooking delicate foods over softly simmering water allows more control than cooking directly over the heat source, where they can get scorched. It allows you to cook over the lowest heat possible, especially when tempering chocolate. Make sure to fill the base pot with just enough water so it doesn't touch the bottom of the inset bowl.

Ice cream maker: Ice cream makers have come a long way since the summer days I used to spend at my Aunt Shirlee's pool. When it was especially hot, she would roll the old-fashioned ice cream machine out of the garage and fill the moat around its throat with ice and rock salt, then we would take turns cranking the tank until our arms were cramping and each sweet chunk of fresh peach was enveloped in thick, icy cream.
Today's machines are far more reasonably sized and priced and require no laborious hand churning. An insulated canister fits over a motorized base and slowly rotates, moving a plastic blade through the cream as it thickens and freezes. Make sure to fully chill your custard or sorbet base before pouring it into the machine; otherwise the insulated canister will thaw from the heat, preventing the contents from freezing sufficiently. The most effortless approach to making ice cream is by spreading the steps out over two or three days: Prepare the base or custard on the first day, then pop it into the fridge. On the second day, pour the base into the ice cream maker. At the point of soft-serve, transfer the semifrozen cream to a covered plastic container and freeze for several hours or overnight.

Ice water bath: I'm not referring to the basin used for soaking sore toes here, although many have been used for such a purpose at my house. An ice water bath is one of those very effective culinary tools that everyone has in their kitchen but rarely thinks of using. Simply a bowl filled with ice and water, an ice water bath is a practical device for cooling hot foods quickly, which is important not just for saving energy in your refrigerator, but for safety, as some foods that cool gradually at room temperature are more prone to growing potentially dangerous bacteria than those that are chilled quickly. Since metal conducts cold temperatures better than glass or plastic, submerge hot liquids right in their copper pans, or stainless pots or bowls, then transfer to storage containers when they are cool.

Measuring cups and spoons: Here is a case where function is more important than price: basic plastic or stainless cups and spoons are just as efficient as those that are more expensive or decorative. Remember to always measure dry ingredients by filling the spoon or cup to the rim, then running the straight edge of a knife across the top to level it off.

Microwave oven: While I wouldn't bake a cake or steam a pudding in a microwave, they are especially handy for melting chocolate and butter and reheating sauces. The temperatures of different ovens can vary dramatically, though, so always err on the side of caution when using the power and time settings until you get used the strength of your particular oven. Microwaves can also cook unevenly—if you don't watch closely you may find that your chocolate is sizzling in one corner while still hard in another. Stir or shake up your ingredients once or twice during cooking to ensure even heat distribution.

Pastry bag: I used to think of pastry bags as being like rights of passage into the world of real baking, as my first pair of pointe shoes was the first step to real ballet dancing. Only serious bakers and perfectionists used them, or those aspiring to becoming one or the other. Luckily, not all tricks of the trade require years of training, and in the case of pastry bags, at least, you don't need to master the technique to look like an artist. Pastry bags can make messy or awkward jobs like administering fillings into tarts or batters into tins fast and easy. Piping meringue for baked Alaska or even pushing store-bought icing through a pastry bag will give a professional look to your dessert. The most pedestrian of cakes will have added flair when topped with a decorative spiral of icing. Once they've added that all-important final touch to a dessert, pastry bags do require a a good wipe with a soapy sponge to clean. Let dry naturally by propping the inverted bag on a bottle or the faucet. If the task at hand is just administering fillings, make a disposable bag by filling a resealable plastic bag with your batter, filling, or whipped cream, then snip off one small corner with scissors. Pipe away, then toss the bag in the trash—no mess, no clean up.

Pastry brush: Buy several pastry brushes, separating those you use for savory cooking from those used for desserts, since they tend to retain food odors and tastes. Wash with warm, soapy water and prop in a glass to dry naturally.

Powdered sugar (also called confectioners' or icing sugar): The basis for many cake frostings, this is finely ground sugar to which cornstarch (cornflour) has been added. I keep a small dispenser with a screw-top sieve filled at all times, so it's always ready to shake over desserts for a finishing touch.

Silpat: Made in France, these rubbery nonstick sheets are modern kitchen super-heroes. They can go from oven to freezer, are microwavable and reusable, and vastly facilitate candy-making, fancy garnishes, and removing sticky baked goods like lacy toffee cookies from pans. Place a sheet of Silpat on a baking tray as you would waxed or parchment paper. No more greasing of baking sheets is needed. Wash with a damp cloth and soapy water and let dry naturally.

Sugar: Use standard granulated table sugar unless otherwise specified.

Simple syrup combines equal parts sugar and water, turning your sugar into liquid and adding sweetness with the grainy texture melted away. Simple syrup is used for sweetening drinks (although superfine sugar works well, too) and frozen desserts like sorbets and granitas.

SIMPLE SYRUP
1 cup sugar
1 cup water

Stir the water and sugar over low heat until the sugar has dissolved, then bring to a simmer and cook for 10 minutes, until syrupy. Let cool and store in a plastic container with a tight cover in the refrigerator.

Superfine sugar: Granulated sugar that is ground finer than regular table sugar dissolves more quickly in liquids and will incorporate more smoothly into desserts based on whipped egg whites, like angel food cake or billowy clouds of Pavlova. You can make superfine sugar at home by placing a few cups of granulated sugar in a food processor fitted with a metal blade and processing for 2 to 3 minutes.

Suprème: This is a classic term for the technique of cutting citrus fruit into sections, with the pith and membranes removed. It is typically used for fruit garnishes or salads. (A similar term, suprème, refers to the technique for splaying open boneless chicken breasts.) To suprème your fruit, top and tail the ends (cut off the top and bottom so the fruit won't roll on your work surface), then cut the sides in downward motions along the peel, so the pith and rind are removed. Cut in between the membranes with a sharp knife to remove the segments.

Torch or hand-held gas flame: I was given one of those little torches for making crème brûlée for Christmas one year, and it was the last time I ever melted sugar under the broiler. Although a regular blowtorch from a hardware store is far more powerful and holds much more gas, either kind allows more control than an oven better for achieving a perfect golden crust on sugar-coated custards or adding just the right amount of burnished brown to meringue desserts.

Vanilla: There are four main producers of vanilla beans around the world: Madagascar, Mexico, Tahiti, and Indonesia. The beans from the different regions vary slightly in appearance but dramatically in nuance of flavor, depending on their area of origin.
Madagascar, which produces what is known as Bourbon vanilla, is the largest producer, with beans that are creamy and sweet-tasting. Bourbon Vanilla is often used for flavoring ice cream and sauces.
Mexican vanilla beans tend to be more spicy, complementing custards like Mexican flan and desserts flavored with cinnamon.
Tahitian vanilla is my vanilla of choice, not only for its wonderfully fragrant floral notes and fruity flavor, but

because cakes and tarts made with it taste more like those found in Parisian bakeries. Vanilla beans from Tahiti are the choice of most high-quality pastry makers in France. Indonesian vanilla tends to be used mostly by commercial bakers for items like packaged cookies, and has a woody, harsh flavor. I don't recommend it for home baking.

Zest: Zesting refers to removing only the outer colored part of a citrus fruit. The zest contains the essential oil and flavor of the fruit, whereas the pith, or the white part, tends to be slightly bitter. Make sure you wash and dry your fruit thoroughly before zesting it to remove any pesticides and waxy coating. Most recipes will call for either grated zest or a julienne (very thin strips). The smallest holes of a four-sided box grater are most commonly used for the job of grating, although I usually end up grating my knuckles as well, so I prefer a hand-held grater. Both tools are available at gourmet specialty stores, although the hand-held ones also have the benefit of being much easier to clean. For a julienne, I prefer to suprème the peel (see *Suprème*), carefully paring the white pith off with a very sharp knife.

Zester: This little tool contains 4 to 6 sharp-rimmed holes on one end for scraping against the rind of citrus fruits. Use a zester when you want thin strands rather than the shreds of grated zest you get from a box grater.

Conversion Chart

Oven Temperatures

F	=	C	=	Gas
250		120		½
275		140		1
300		150		2
325		160		3
350		180		4
375		190		5
400		200		6
425		220		7
450		230		8
475		240		9
500		260		10

Measures

US	=	Metric
¼ tsp		1.25 ml
½ tsp		2.5 ml
1 tsp		5 ml
1 T (3 tsp)		15 ml
2 T (1 fl oz)		30 ml
¼ c		60 ml
$\frac{1}{3}$ c		80 ml
½ c		125 ml
1 c		240 ml
1 pt (2 c)		480 ml
1 qt (4 c)		960 ml
1 gal (4 qts)		3.84 liters

½ ounce	15 grams
4 ounces	110 grams
8 ounces	230 grams
1 pound	454 grams
2.2 pounds	1 kilogram

Length

US	=	Metric
$\frac{1}{8}$ inch		3 mm
¼ inch		5 mm
½ inch		1 cm
1 inch		2.5 cm

BIBLIOGRAPHY

Anderson, Jack, *The Nutcracker Ballet* (Mayflower Books, 1979)
Balanchine, George, and Francis Mason, *101 Stories of the Great Ballets* (Anchor Books, 1975)
Collister, Linda, *Chocolate* (Ryland, Peters & Small, 2002)
Dunning, Jennifer, *"But first a school."* (Viking Penguin, 1985)
Hoffmann, E.T.A., *The Best Tales of Hoffmann* (Dover Publications, 1967)

Thank you to:
Yves Averous, Noah Gelber, Stephan Laurent and Butler University, Jean Weaver and Mary Ann Gebara of Nutcracker of Middle Georgia, Bruce Stievel of Nevada Ballet Theatre, and Christopher Rankin.

For my littlest sweet Alex.

Index